GLUTEN FREE & VEGETARIAN
TASTES OF SPAIN
COOKBOOK

A DEFINITIVE GUIDE TO A GRANDMA'S HOME COOKING

Marta Ortiz

Text, photography and design: Marta Ortiz

Copyright © 2023
Marta Ortiz
All rights reserved
ISBN 9798852128539

Editing & proofreading:
Alun Jones

TABLE OF CONTENTS

SPANISH GASTRONOMY & TAPAS   ❋ APT FOR VEGANS

VEGETABLES
- RUSSIAN POTATO SALAD 8
- ❋ CUCUMBER & PEPPER SALAD - PIPIRRANA 10
- ❋ LETTUCE HEARTS TOPPED WITH VINAGRETTE 10
- ❋ LA MANCHA PISTO 11
- ❋ ROASTED VEGETABLES – ESCALIVADA 12
- ❋ MALLORCAN VEGETABLE TUMBET 14
- ❋ VEGETABLE STEW NAVARRAN STYLE – MENESTRA 16
- BATTERED EGGPLANT WITH HONEY/AGAVE 18
- ❋ CABBAGE NAVARRAN STYLE 20
- ❋ WRINKLED POTATOES WITH 2 DIPS 22
- IMPORTANT POTATOES 24

SPOON DISHES
- ❋ COLD TOMATO SOUP – GAZPACHO 28
- ❋ SALMOREJO 29
- ❋ ALMOND AND GARLIC CREME - AJO BLANCO 30
- ❋ LENTIL STEW 31
- ❋ LENT CHICKPEA STEW 32
- ❋ WHITE BEAN STEW 33
- ❋ GARLIC SOUP CASTILLIAN STYLE 34
- MUSHROOM CREAMY SOUP 35
- ❋ ZUCCHINI CREAMY SOUP 36
- ❋ LEEK SOUP – PORRUSALDA 37

PASTA & RICE
- CLAY DISH - GREIXONERA 40
- ❋ PASTA GARLIC STYLE 42
- PENNE WITH FUNGHI & CHEESE 42
- ❋ VEGETABLE PAELLA 44
- ❋ POTATOES WITH RICE 46
- CUBAN STYLE RICE 48

EGGS
- SPANISH POTATO OMELETTE 50
- BROKEN EGGS 52
- CARLISTAS EGGS 54
- OPENED EGGS WITH GREEN ASPARAGUS 56
- MUSHROOM & GREEN ASPARAGUS SCRAMBLED EGGS 57
- GIRALDA EGGS 58

TAPAS

- ✦ MUSHROOMS GARLIC STYLE 60
- ✦ STUFFED MUSHROOMS WITH SPINACH AND PINE NUTS 61
- ✦ BREAD & TOMATO 62
- ZUCCHINI & MUSHROOM TOAST 63
- GOAT CHEESE AND TOMATO JAM TAPA 64
- GOAT CHEESE, CARAMELIZED ONION AND WALNUTS TAPA.................. 64
- MUSHROOM, BECHAMEL AND GRILLED CHEESE TOAST 65
- BRAVE POTATOES 66
- FUNGHI CROQUETTES 68
- MANCHEGO CHEESE CROQUETTES 70
- SPINACH CROQUETTES 70

DESSERTS

- SANTIAGO CAKE 72
- OLIVE OIL AND YOGURT SPONGE CAKE 74
- SPANISH SWEET BREAD – TORRIJAS 74
- FRIED MILK - LECHE FRITA 76
- CANTABRIAN CHEESECAKE 78
- ALMOND COOKIES - ALMENDRADOS 80
- MARZIPAN 81
- CLASSIC PANELLETS 82
- PANELLETS WITH PINENUTS 82
- PANELLETS WITH CHOPPED ALMONDS 82
- COCONUT PANELLETS 84
- COFFEE PANELLETS 84
- LITTLE SIGHS - MERENGUITOS 85
- ALMOND SIGHS 86
- FLAN 88
- SPANSIH CUSTARD NATILLAS 88
- CATALAN BURNT CRÈME - CREMA CATALANA 89

REFERENCE RECIPES

- ✦ VEGETABLE STOCK 92
- MAYONNAISE.. 92
- EGG AIOLI 93
- ✦ GENUINE AIOLI 93
- CLASSIC BECHAMEL... 94
- THICK BECHAMEL 94

- Abbreviations: Tbsp.: tablespoon tsp.: teaspoon
- The garlic cloves should always be peeled in the recipes unless mentioned otherwise.
- All the vegetables have to be washed and deseeded. No need to peel them if they are organic.
- Unless specified, you can choose any type of cheese to grate.

DISCLAIMER: The user of this book is responsible for ensuring a gluten-free cooking environment. While every effort has been made to identify and use gluten-free ingredients in the production of this book, the user takes full responsibility for ensuring that those consuming any food produced following the recipes in this book are not intolerant to any of the ingredients included in this book. Under no circumstances shall the author be liable for any direct or indirect incidental, consequential, special or exemplary damages arising out of or in connection with the contents of this book.

SPANISH GASTRONOMY AND TAPAS

In Spain, food is essential part of our everyday lives. As we Spaniards often say. "We live to eat rather than eat to live." Our country is so rich and diverse on every level and we enjoy an outstanding gastronomy with an enormous wide range of foods and culinary traditions. The gastronomy of Spain is well known all over the world, not only for its excellence but for its high health value as a Mediterranean diet. But it's not only about the food itself. Going out for a "tapeo" (to have tapas), meeting up for an "aperitivo", these are ordinary social activities that revolve around food and literally bring Spanish food alive.

My intention with this cookbook is to introduce you to over 60 authentic gluten free and vegetarian Spanish recipes from different regions of Spain and share our traditions, the origins of the recipes and how and when we usually prepare them. In two words: our "culinary culture".

In some of the recipes, you will see a symbol that says "Also a Tapa". This means that you can also serve it in small portions and eat it as a Tapa. But what is a Tapa?, you may ask. The word Tapa comes from the Spanish verb "tapar" which means to cover. It is said that it all started in Andalusia when people who were drinking outdoors came up with the idea of covering their drinks with a slice of bread between sips to keep the flies out of their glass. Tapas have since evolved considerably and now there are several different categories but with one essential thing in common: you must be able to hold them in one hand or eat them in two to three bites. A tapa may be called a pincho in one region of Spain or a montadito in another.

TAPAS SUB-CLASSES:

- Pinchos (Pintxos in Northern Spain refer to any type of tapa): This is a tapa with a pincho or toothpick through the middle to keep all the ingredients aligned and together. Most of the time, the base is a slice of bread, but not always. The toothpick also helps keep track of the number of tapas the customer has eaten.
- Banderillas: Small skewer Tapas.
- Montaditos (On top): the base is one or more slices of bread with other ingredients placed on top.
- Cazuelitas (Clay dishes): served in a small clay dish.
- Raciones (Portions): a small plate with a batch of croquettes, squid rings, brave potatoes, potato salad, etc, which can be shared (or not).

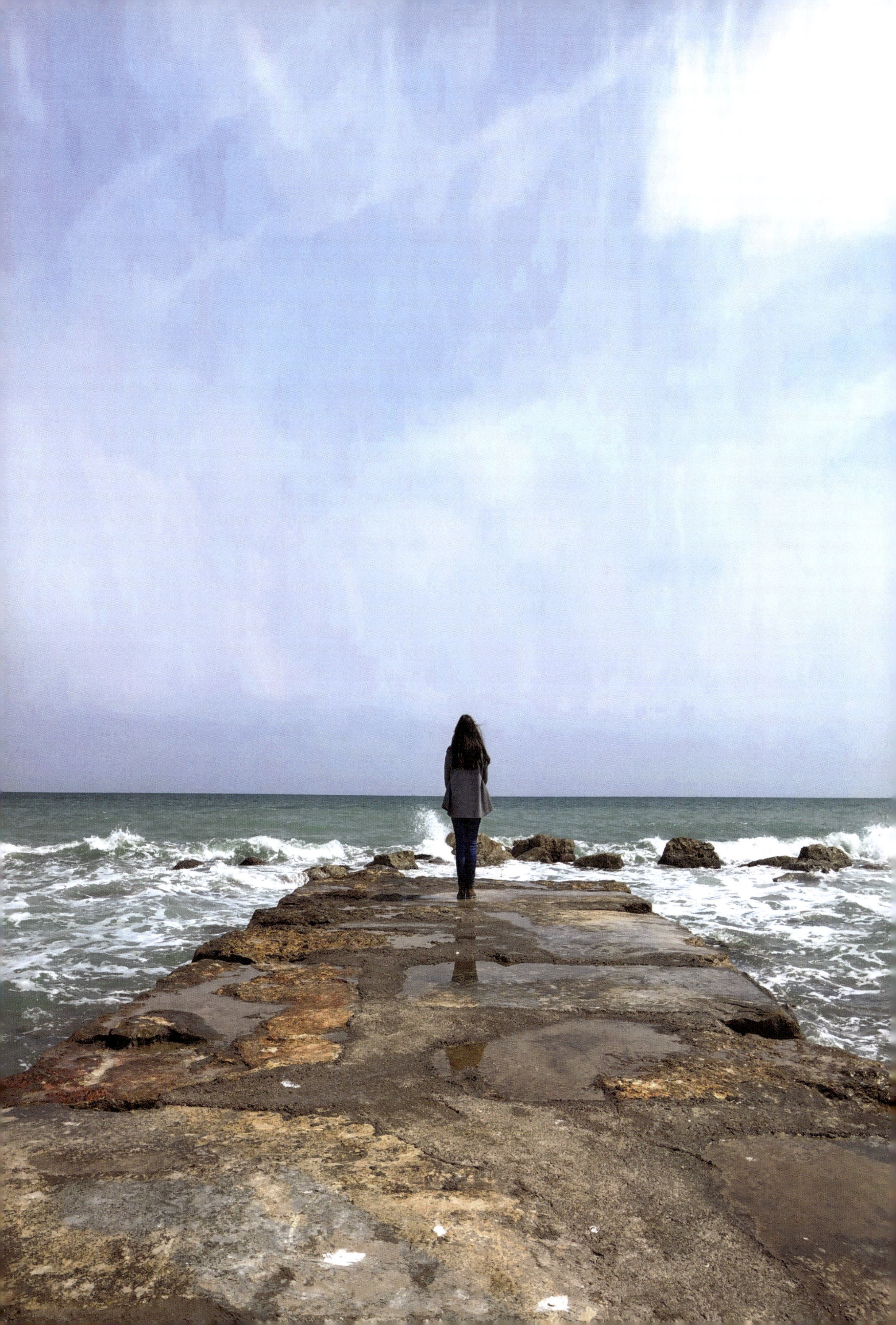

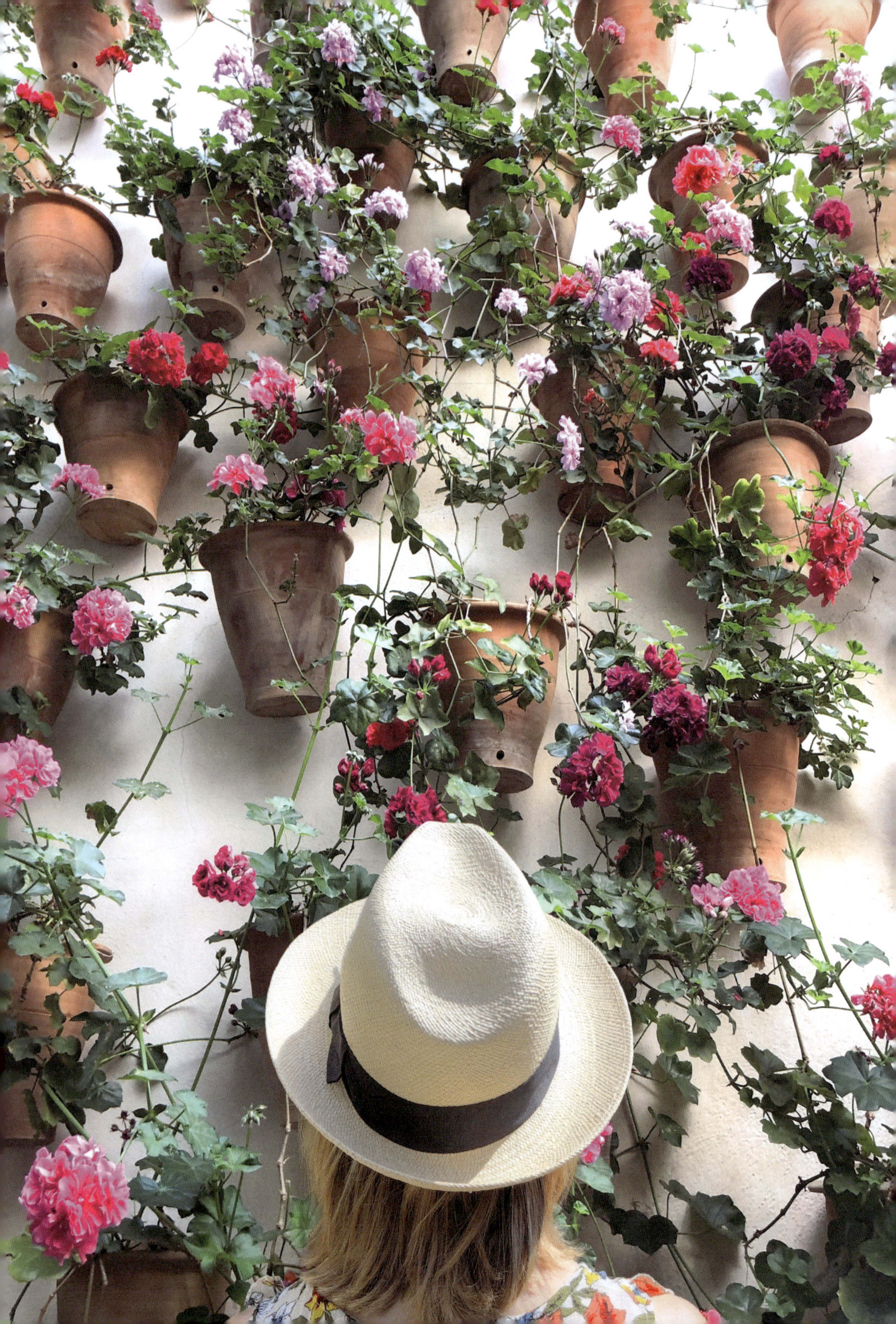

Vegetables

VEGETABLES

RUSSIAN POTATO SALAD Ensaladilla Rusa

This recipe dates back to the 19th century, when a Belgian chef, Lucien Olivier, who worked at the Muscovite Restaurant l'Ermitage, invented this salad, which was a great success among the Russian aristocracy. His sous-chef copied this successful recipe and took it with him to another restaurant but that version didn't have much success. Nevertheless, that copy served as a basis for today's recipe, which has become so popular that it has been included in the national Spanish gastronomy.

SERVES 4-6 AS A STARTER OR 10-12 AS A TAPA:
450 gr. (15.5 oz.) potatoes
2 large carrots (180gr./6 oz.)
100 gr. (3.5 oz.) frozen peas
1 hardboiled egg
350 ml. (1 ½ cup) mayonnaise (recipe on page 92)
salt to taste
For Decoration:
6-8 green or/and black olives
4-6 roasted red pepper strips
1 hardboiled egg

1. Peel and wash the potatoes and carrots. Cut the potatoes into small square dices about 2 cm. (1 inch) and the carrots into 3 mm. (1/9 inch) thick slices. Then, cut the carrot slices in half.

2. Bring a pot with water and 1 Tbsp. of salt to the boil. Add the potatoes and simmer for 8 minutes. Add in the carrots and peas. Bring into a boil and then lower the heat to simmer for 12-15 min. or until vegetables are tender. Take all the vegetables out with a slotted spoon and place them into a strainer. Store the water as vegetable stock for another recipe.

3. Boil 2 eggs. Finely chop one egg and slice the other one for decoration.

4. When the vegetables in the strainer are cooled, place them in a large tray or plate. Mix in the chopped egg.

5. Add the mayonnaise (homemade recipe on page 92). You can either spread a thick layer of mayonnaise on top or you can mix it until well combined with all the ingredients. Use the olives, egg slices and pepper strips as decoration on top. Refrigerate for at least 3 hours covered with cling film. Serve cold but take out of the fridge 15 minutes before serving.

TIP: You can use more ingredients such as sliced or chopped fresh tomatoes, chopped fresh lettuce, boiled corn or even boiled green beans

ALSO A TAPA

CUCUMBER AND PEPPER SALAD Pipirrana

This recipe originally comes from Jaén, an Andalusian region in Southern Spain. It's halfway between a salad and a gazpacho. It's mostly eaten during Summer because it is very refreshing. You can find different versions across Spain. Here I'll show you the original recipe.

SERVES 4
1 large cucumber
1 large green pepper
1 large red pepper
Spanish extra Virgin olive oil
½ tsp. apple vinegar
chives for decoration

1. Wash all the vegetables. Peel and deseed the cucumber and tomatoes if you want.

2. Finely dice all the vegetables and combine in a large bowl. Pour 3 Tbsp. of olive oil, ½ tsp. of vinegar all over the ingredients. Season with salt.

3. Decorate with chives. Serve cold.

LETTUCE HEARTS TOPPED WITH VINAGRETTE
Cogollos a la vinagreta

This Navarran classic uses lettuce hearts as main ingredient. The ones from Tudela (a nice little town on the banks of the Ebro river) have a very characteristic flavor ideal for this dish. However, any lettuce hearts will do as long as they are good quality.

SERVES 4:
2 lettuce hearts
½ green bell pepper
½ red bell pepper
1 spring onion
1 Tbsp. apple vinegar
3-4 Tbsp. Spanish extra Virgin olive oil
 salt to taste

1. Wash the lettuce hearts. Cut in quarters. Dry them by squeezing them carefully or shaking them off.

2. Wash and finely mince all the vegetables. Place them in a bowl and pour in the oil. Stir with a fork to combine all ingredients well. Place the lettuce hearts on a plate or platter. Season each lettuce heart with salt and ground pepper to taste. Spoon the bowl contents all over the lettuce hearts.

VEGETABLES

LA MANCHA PISTO Pisto Manchego

This recipe from Castilla la Mancha is one of the most well-known and popular vegetable dishes in Spain. It is very similar to the French "Ratatouille" and the Italian "Caponata". It has different ingredients depending on the region and the taste of the cook, but it should always have at least tomato, zucchini, pepper and onion among its ingredients.

SERVES 4:
400 gr. (13 oz.) courgettes/zucchini
2 red bell peppers
2 green bell peppers
1 large onion
400 gr. (13 oz.) ripe red tomatoes
2-3 Tbsp. Spanish extra Virgin olive oil
salt to taste
1 tsp. brown sugar

1. Wash all the vegetables. Peel and deseed the tomatoes. Cut all the vegetables into small dices, although you can cut the peppers into stripes if you prefer.

2. Heat 2-3 Tbsp. of olive oil in a large pan over a medium heat. When the oil is hot, turn down to low-medium heat and fry the peppers and onion until tender but not completely cooked (about 5-6 minutes) stirring occasionally. Add in the courgettes/zucchini and fry until all ingredients are tender and cooked (around 6-7 minutes).

3. Fold in the tomatoes. Sprinkle brown sugar all over the tomatoes to get rid of their acidity. Season with salt, stir and simmer for 15 minutes with a lid on the pan.

ROASTED VEGETABLES Escalivada

Escalivada is a straightforward vegetable dish that originates from the Catalonian region of Spain. The Catalan word "escalivar" means to roast over ashes or embers. But nowadays, it's usually cooked in an oven with very good results.

SERVES 2:
1 large eggplant
1 large red bell pepper
1 medium onion
salt to taste
Spanish extra Virgin olive oil
1 minced garlic clove (optional)

1. Pre-heat the oven to 180°C (350°F). Line a large roasting pan with baking paper. Peel the onions. Wash the eggplants, onions and red peppers. Place them on the paper. Cut off the eggplant tails.

2. Make a cross shaped cut with a knife on the bottom of each eggplant. Pour a splash of olive oil all over the vegetables. Roast in oven on middle rack for about 1h 15m, turning over the vegetables every 30 minutes or so. If any vegetables, particularly peppers become thoroughly cooked, while need more time, remove from tray and continue roasting the rest. Remove from oven and allow to cool.

3. Peel the eggplants when they are cool enough to handle with your hands. Peel the peppers with your hands and discard seeds and stems. Press them all in your hands so the water in them comes out. Cut lengthwise into strips. Place them on a platter or tray.

4. Remove the hard outer layer of the onions. Cut off the edges of the onions if they are black. Cut them into strips and transfer onto the same platter or tray with the rest of vegetables. Pour over a splash of oil and season with salt. You can also sprinkle minced or crushed garlic clove. Serve at room temperature.

TIP: Place some escalivada on top of a gluten-free toast if you prefer to have it as a very nice tapa

ALSO A TAPA

MALLORCAN TUMBET   Tumbet Mallorquín

This recipe originally comes from the Balearic Island of Mallorca and it was a way to use up the surplus of seasonal vegetables. It can be eaten on its own as a first course or as a side dish. Originally, the eggplant wasn't peeled for this recipe, but nowadays, many people peel it.

SERVES 4:
1 kg. (2.2 lb.) ripe peeled tomatoes
2 large eggplants
2 large green peppers
1 onion cut into rings
300 gr. (10.5 oz) potatoes
salt to taste
2 tsp. brown sugar
Spanish extra virgin olive oil

1. Cut the eggplants crosswise into thin round slices. Leave them to soak in a bowl of salted water for 30 min. to get rid of the bitterness. Wash and dry the slices. Fry them in hot oil and set aside on a plate lined with kitchen roll.

2. You don't have to peel the potatoes if they are Bio. Cut them into thin round slices and wash under cold water. Dry them and season with salt. Fry in hot oil and set aside on a plate lined with kitchen roll.

3. Cut the green peppers lengthwise into 1 cm. (1/3 inch) thick strips. Fry in the same oil where you fried the potatoes until tender. Set aside like before.

4. Fry the onion in the same oil until it looks translucent. Add the finely diced tomatoes and pour 50 ml. (1.8 fl. oz.) water. Season with salt to taste and 2 tsp. brown sugar to get rid of the tomato acidity. Simmer gently uncovered until the sauce has reduced. You can pass the sauce through a sieve if you want. Set aside.

5. Use a deep oven tray to assemble the dish: Place a bit of the tomato sauce and then a layer of the peppers. Put on top more sauce and then a layer of potatoes, more sauce and then a layer of eggplants and so forth until you use up all ingredients.

6. Bake in pre-heated oven at 190ªC (375ªF) for 15 minutes on middle rack and serve immediately.

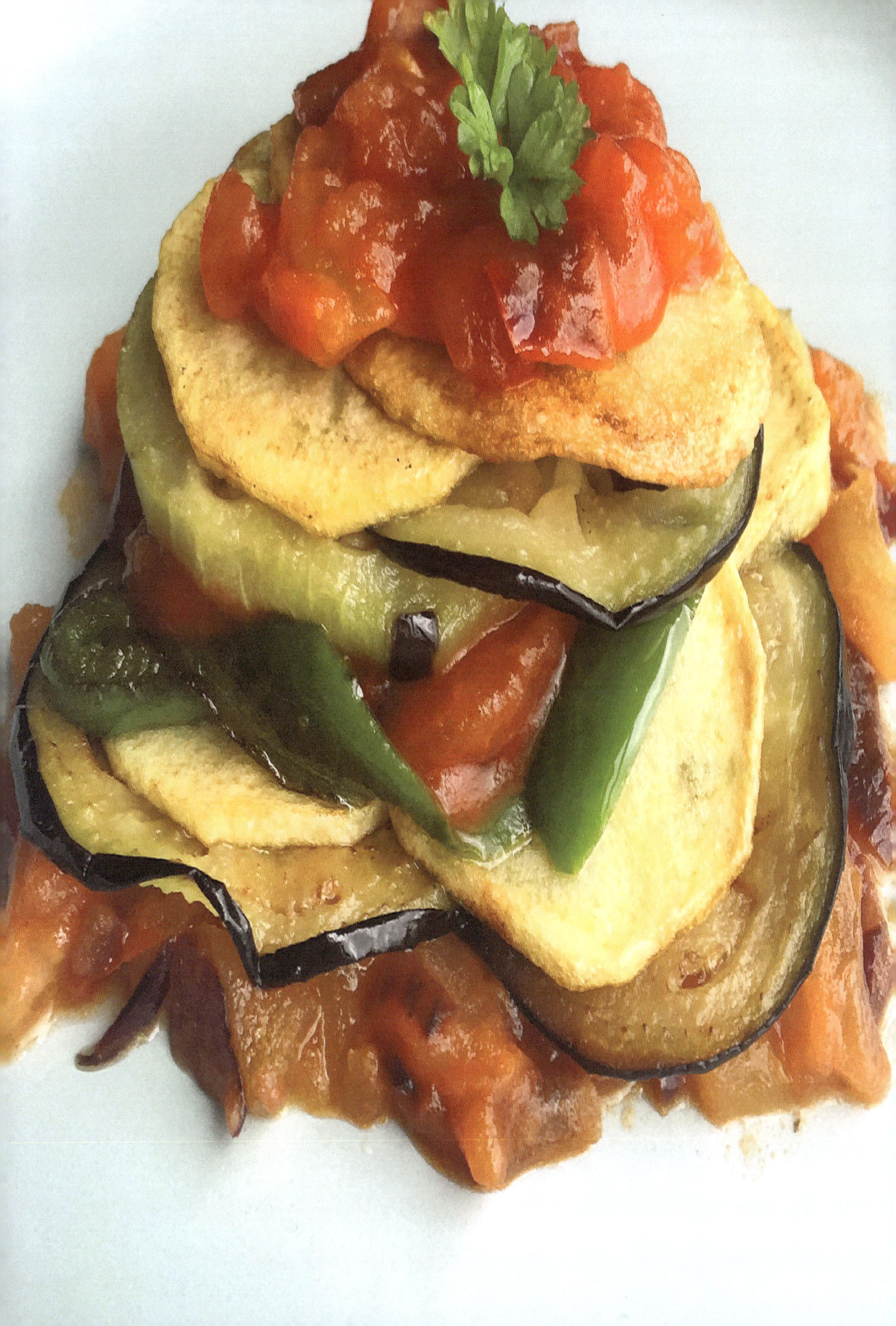

VEGETABLE STEW NAVARRAN STYLE Menestra

You can add or substitute any vegetable you like as there's no exact recipe and it can be prepared at any time of the year. The most famous Menestra is the one from the Navarra region. It's usually served as a starter and sometimes potatoes are added to make it more complete.

SERVES 4:
1 medium onion, finely minced
5-6 artichoke hearts
3 Tbsp. Spanish extra Virgin olive oil
200 gr. (6.5 oz.) green beans
3 carrots finely sliced
120 gr. (4.2 oz.) peas
6 white asparagus (optional)
salt to taste
more optional vegetables: Brussels sprouts, green asparagus, cauliflower and/or broccoli florets

1. Prepare each artichoke. Cut off most of the stalk with a sharp knife. Trim away the top of the artichoke bulb (approx. the top third). Tear off the lower and tougher outer leaves until the yellowy-green center is exposed. With a small sharp knife, trim the tough parts around the stalk. Cut lengthwise into quarters or into smaller chunks.

2. Use a carrot peeler to take off the outer layer of the asparagus if using. Wash and boil in water till tender. Set aside.

3. Pour 3 Tbsp. olive oil into a deep-frying pan. Add in and stir fry the artichoke quarters and onion over a medium heat until the onion is translucent.

4. Add the rest of the vegetables, except the asparagus. Give it a good stir. Cover with a lid and simmer over a medium-low heat, stirring occasionally until all vegetables are tender (about 20-25 min.). Stir in the asparagus 5 min. before finishing. If you see it gets too dry, add a little bit of water to prevent the ingredients from burning.

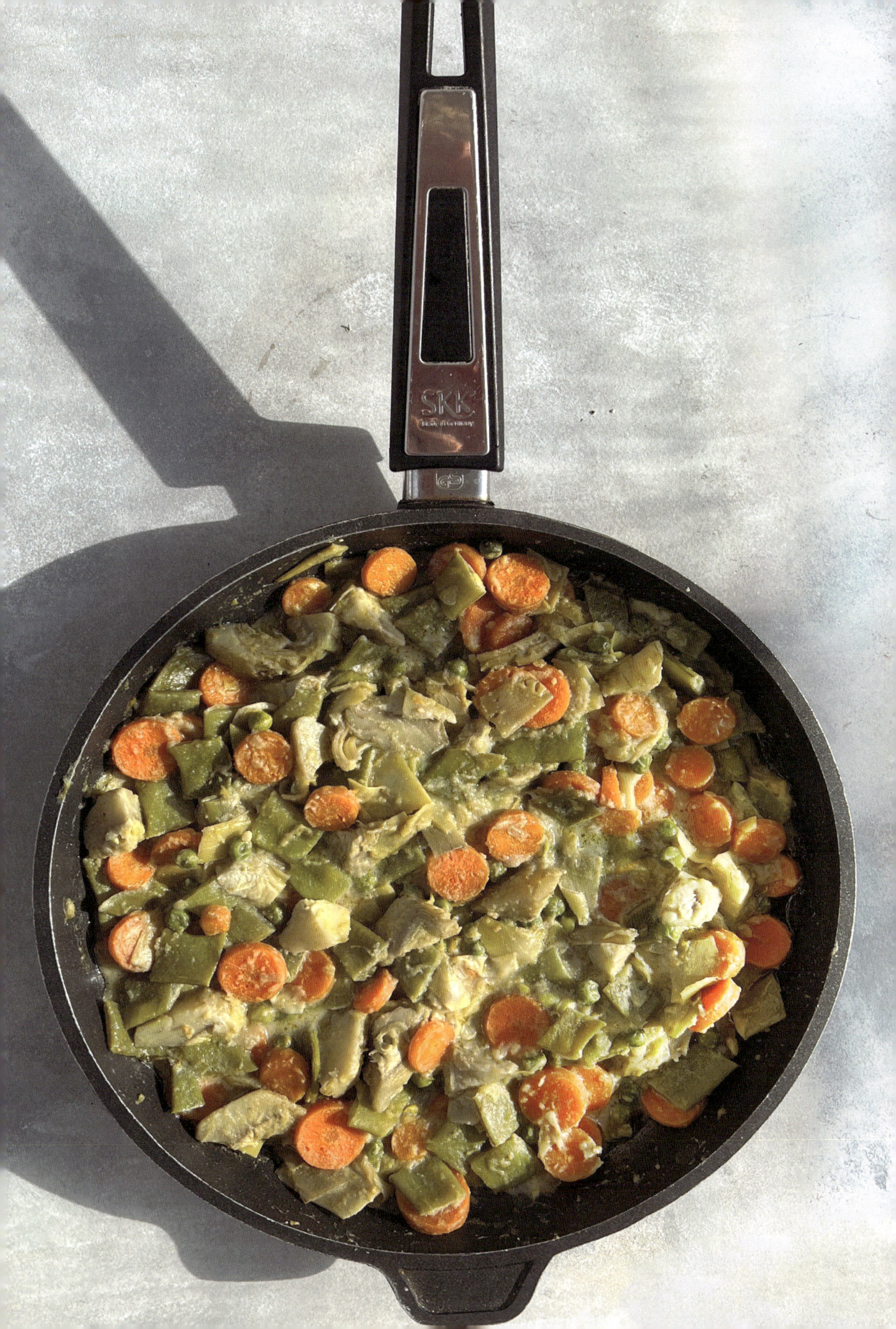
SKK

FRIED EGGPLANT WITH HONEY/AGAVE
Berenjenas fritas con miel/ágave

This is a typical recipe form the Andalusian region. You can have it as a side dish or as a tapa.

SERVES 4:
1 large or 2 small eggplants
3 Tbsp. buckwheat flour
3 Tbsp. chickpea flour
1 beaten egg
Spanish Virgil olive oil
Honey/agave
black pepper
salt to taste

1. Wash the eggplants and cut into into 1 cm. (1/3 inch) thick round slices. You could also cut them into sticks. Place them in a bowl or container and cover them with water and 1 Tbsp. of salt. Leave in for 30 minutes in order for the salted water to draw out the eggplant bitterness. Then, take the eggplant slices out and rinse under tap water. Dry with a paper towel and set aside.

2. Mix the buckwheat and chickpea flour and place in a bowl or plate. Make sure the eggplant slices are dry and coat each slice with the flour mix, shaking off any excess.

3. Roll the slices on a plate with 1 beaten egg so they are completely coated.

4. Heat up a good amount of olive oil in a non-stick frying pan. The oil must cover the bottom half of the slices and be quite hot at first. When it's hot (but before getting smoky hot) place them carefully in the oil. Lower the heat to a medium heat. Fry them in small batches. Turn them gently, for about 2 minutes, or until they are golden on both sides and tender.

5. Using a slotted spoon, lift them out, holding them briefly over the pan to allow the excess oil to drain. Transfer to a plate lined with kitchen roll to drain further. Season with a pinch of salt and ground pepper. Serve immediately after drizzling honey or molasses on top of the slices.

TIP: You can try this recipe using zucchini and/or extra coating with gluten free breadcrumbs after dipping in beaten eggs

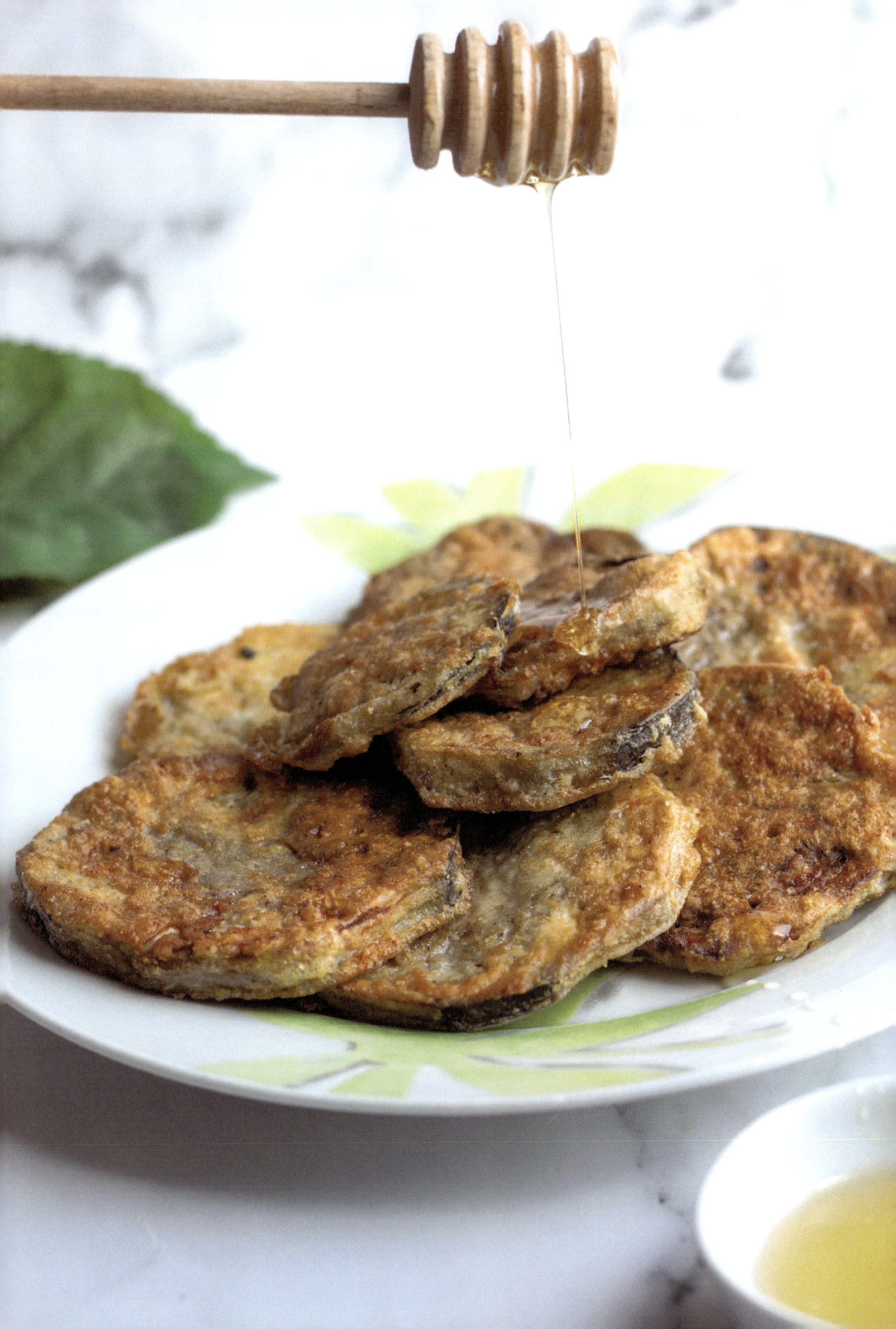

CABBAGE NAVARRAN STYLE Col a la Navarra

It may not sound very appealing but I can assure you this recipe will make you love cabbage if you are not a great fan of this vegetable.

SERVES 4:
1 small cabbage
350 gr. (12.3 oz.) potatoes
8 garlic cloves with skin
8 Tbsp. Spanish Virgin olive oil
salt to taste

1. Cut off the stem of the cabbage. Since its chemicals will react with metal, use a stainless-steel knife to cut it. Remove the outer layer of soggy leaves and cut the cabbage around the core into smaller pieces. Discard the core. Peel away the leaves and rinse them under water. Break them into smaller pieces with your hands. Cut them into strips with a stainless knife. Wash and cut the potatoes into medium chunks.

2. Bring a large pot of water into a boil. Add the cabbage strips and potato chunks. Bring back to a boil and reduce heat to low. Simmer with a lid on for about 40 minutes or until tender.

3. Drain using a colander and set aside. You can use the water where the cabbage was boiled for other recipes such as soups or casseroles.

4. In a large deep-frying pan or pot heat 8 Tbsp. Spanish Virgin olive oil. When hot, stir in the unpeeled garlic cloves and fry until golden on both sides.

5. Stir in the drain cabbage and mix well so the oil coats the cabbage. Season with salt to taste. Lower the heat to minimum heat and simmer covered for 1 hour stirring occasionally. Pour a little bit of water in which you boiled the cabbage if the pan or pot gets too dry.

6. Serve and enjoy.

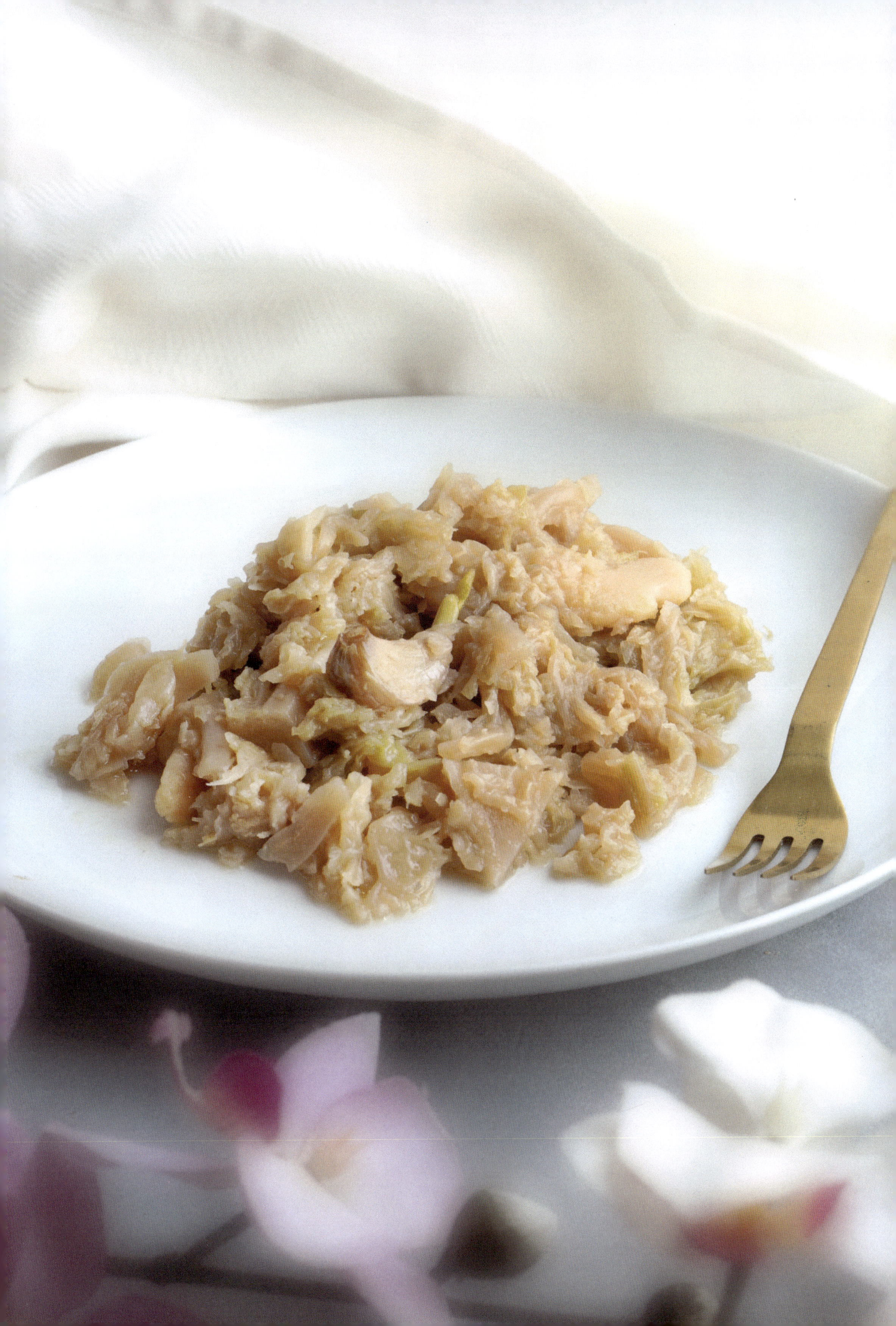

WRINKLED POTATOES WITH 2 DIPS
Papas arrugas con 2 mojos

This is the most well-known recipe from the Canary Islands. The aboriginal people in South America used the name "Papa" to refer to the potato in her native language, the Quechua. So in the Canary islands the original name for the tubercule has been kept.

SERVES 3:
<u>For the potatoes:</u>
500 gr. (1.1 lb.) new potatoes (all small and about the same size)
125 gr. (1/2 cup) rock salt

<u>Red Dip - Mojo Picón:</u>
2 garlic cloves
1 dried cayenne pepper (1 more for a hotter sauce)
½ tsp. sweet smoked paprika
1/4 tsp. ground cumin seeds
salt to taste
1/2 tsp. white wine vinegar
5 Tbsp.) Spanish Virgin olive oil

<u>Green Dip - Mojo Verde:</u>
2 garlic cloves
1/4 tsp. ground cumin seeds
8 gr. (0.28 oz.) freshly minced coriander
salt to taste
1/2 tsp. white wine vinegar
5 Tbsp. Spanish Virgin olive oil

<u>For both dips:</u>

There are two methods:

A. The traditional one using a mortar and a pestle: First, crush the dry ingredients with the pestle until you get a smooth paste. Add the vinegar will stirring. Add the olive oil olive oil slowly into the mortar while you turn the pestle in circular motions to emulsify it.

B. The modern one using a blender with all the ingredients in one go.

<u>For the wrinkled potatoes:</u>

1. Rinse the potatoes off under cold water while scrubbing well with a vegetable brush.

2. Place them in a large pot and cover with enough cold water just to cover the potatoes. Bring to a boil and then lower the heat to medium. Add half the salt. Cook covered with a lid for about 20-25 minutes or until the potatoes are tender.

3. Drain the potatoes, leaving about 3 Tbsp. of water in the pot. Add the other half of the salt. Put the potatoes back into the pot and cook them on a low heat while gently stirring them. A salt crust will start to appear on the bottom of the pan. Continue to stir and cook until their skin starts to wrinkle (about 2 minutes). Remove from the heat and let them rest in the pot before serving with the mojos (dips).

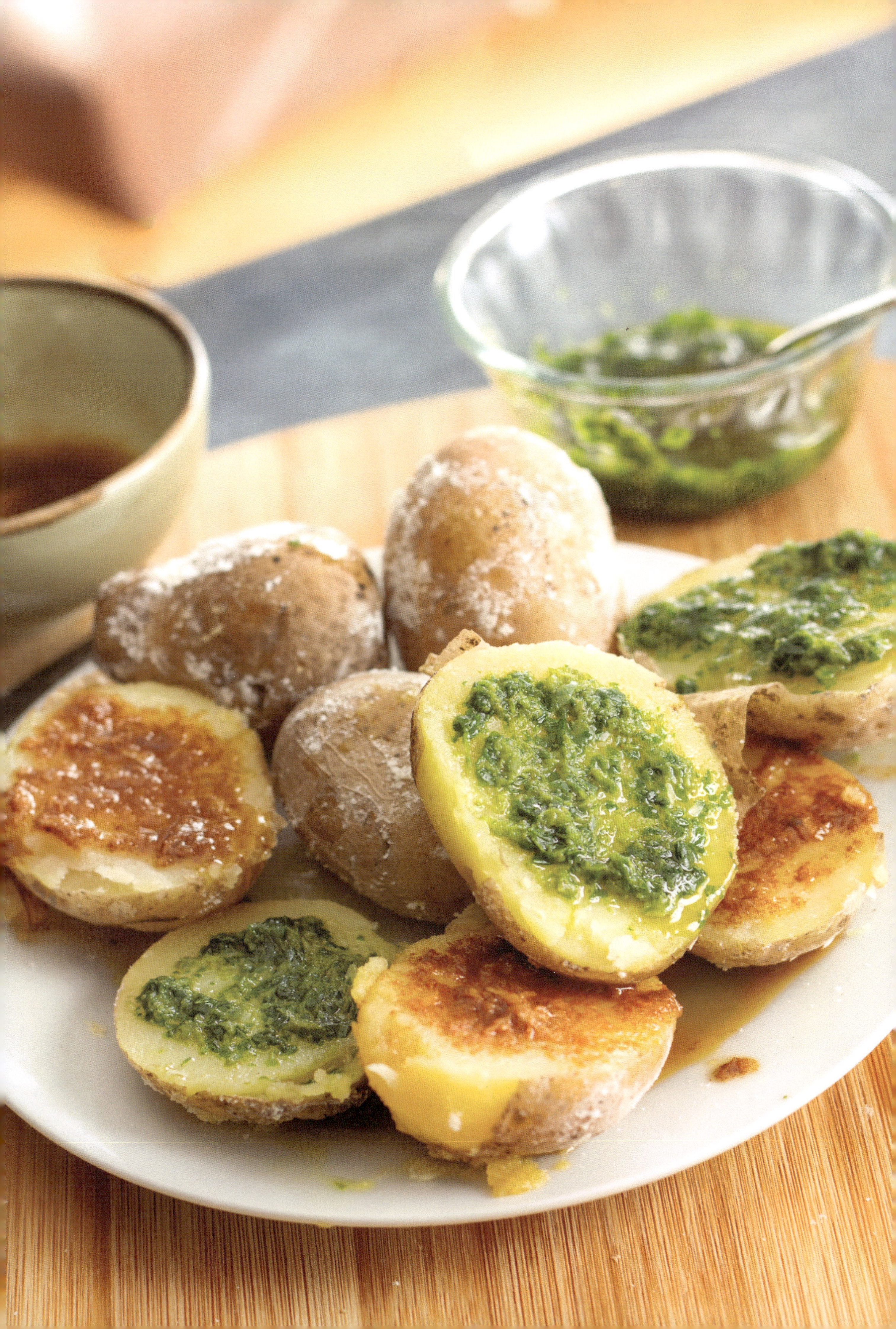

IMPORTANT POTATOES Patatas a la importancia

This is an ancient rural dish that originally comes from the Palencia region of Spain.

SERVES 2-3 PEOPLE:

350 gr. (12.3 oz.) potatoes

Salt to taste

2 Tbsp. Buckwheat flour

2 Tbsp. Chickpea flour

1 beaten egg

1/2 medium onion, finely minced

Spanish Virgin olive oil

1 garlic clove, finely minced

6-8 saffron threads

2 ½ cup vegetable broth

1 Tbsp. freshly minced parsley

1. Wash the potatoes under running water. You don't have to peel them if they are Bio but if you do, <u>do not wash</u> them again. Cut them into 1 cm. (1/3 ich) thick round slices. Make sure they are completely dry. Season with salt.

2. Mix the buckwheat and chickpea flour and place in a bowl or plate. Prepare another plate with the beaten egg.

3. Coat the potato slices completely with the flour mix, shaking off any excess.

4. Dip them in the beaten egg so they get completely coated.

5. Heat up a good amount of olive oil in a non-stick frying pan over a high-medium heat. The amount of oil depends on the size of the pan. The oil must cover the bottom half of the potatoes and be quite hot at first. When it's hot (but before getting smoky hot) place them carefully in the oil. Lower the heat to a medium heat. Fry them in small batches until they are golden on both sides. They will still be hard and not fully cooked. They just need to be golden on the outside.

6. Using a slotted spoon, lift the potatoes out, holding them briefly over the pan to allow excess oil to drain, and transfer to a plate to drain further. They should not be stacked or touching each other so the batter doesn't get ruined.

7. Traditionally, a clay casserole is used buy you can use any type. You can even use a deep pan. Heat up 3 Tbsp. of olive oil and fry the minced onion. When the onion is translucent, stir in the garlic and fresh parsley over medium heat. When the vegetables are done, pour in the vegetable broth and saffron threads. Bring to a gentle boil.

8. Place the potatoes carefully in the casserole. If the broth doesn't cover completely the potatoes, add some more broth until they are covered. Simmer with a lid on over a medium-low heat for 30 minutes or until the potatoes are tender. Serve immediately.

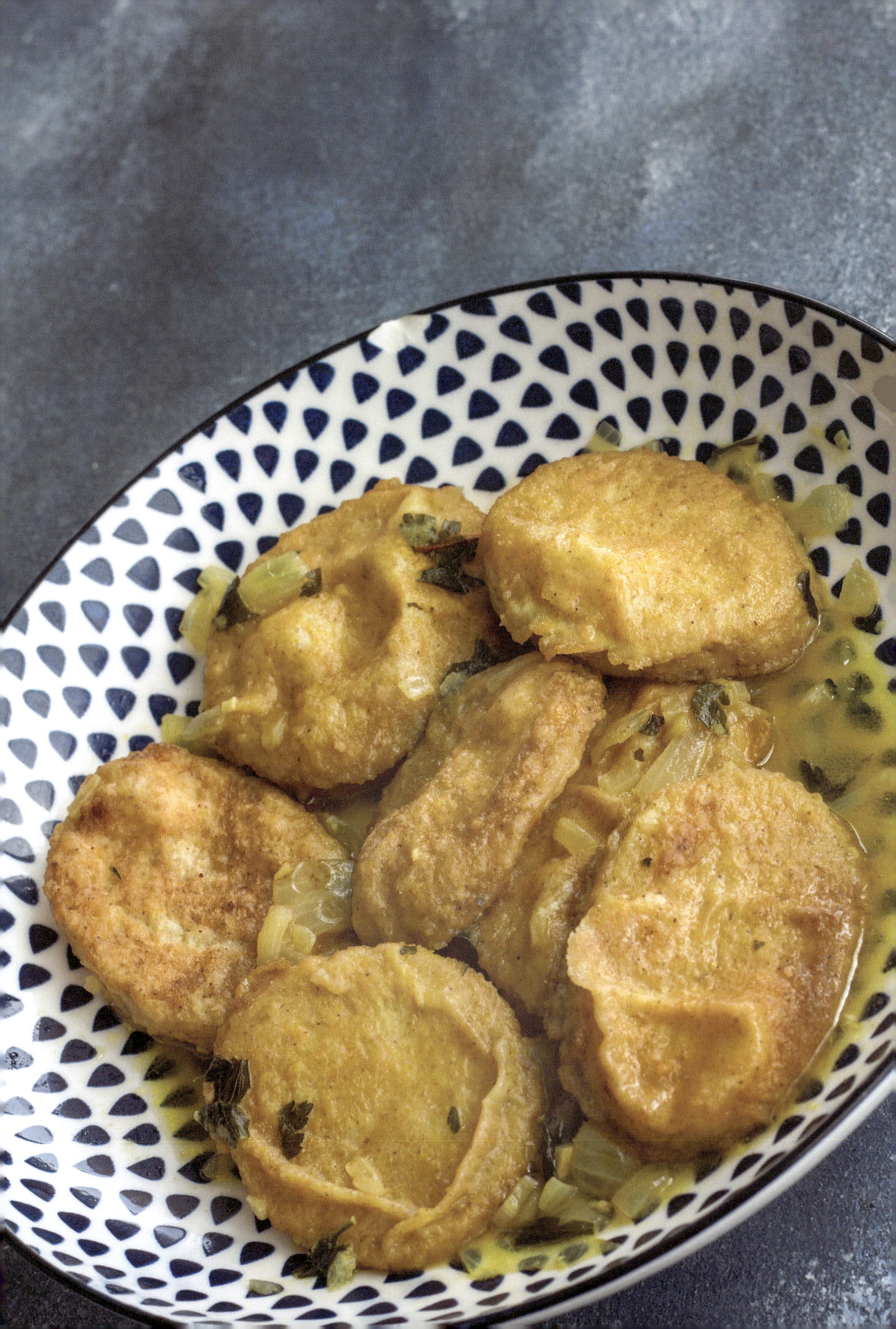

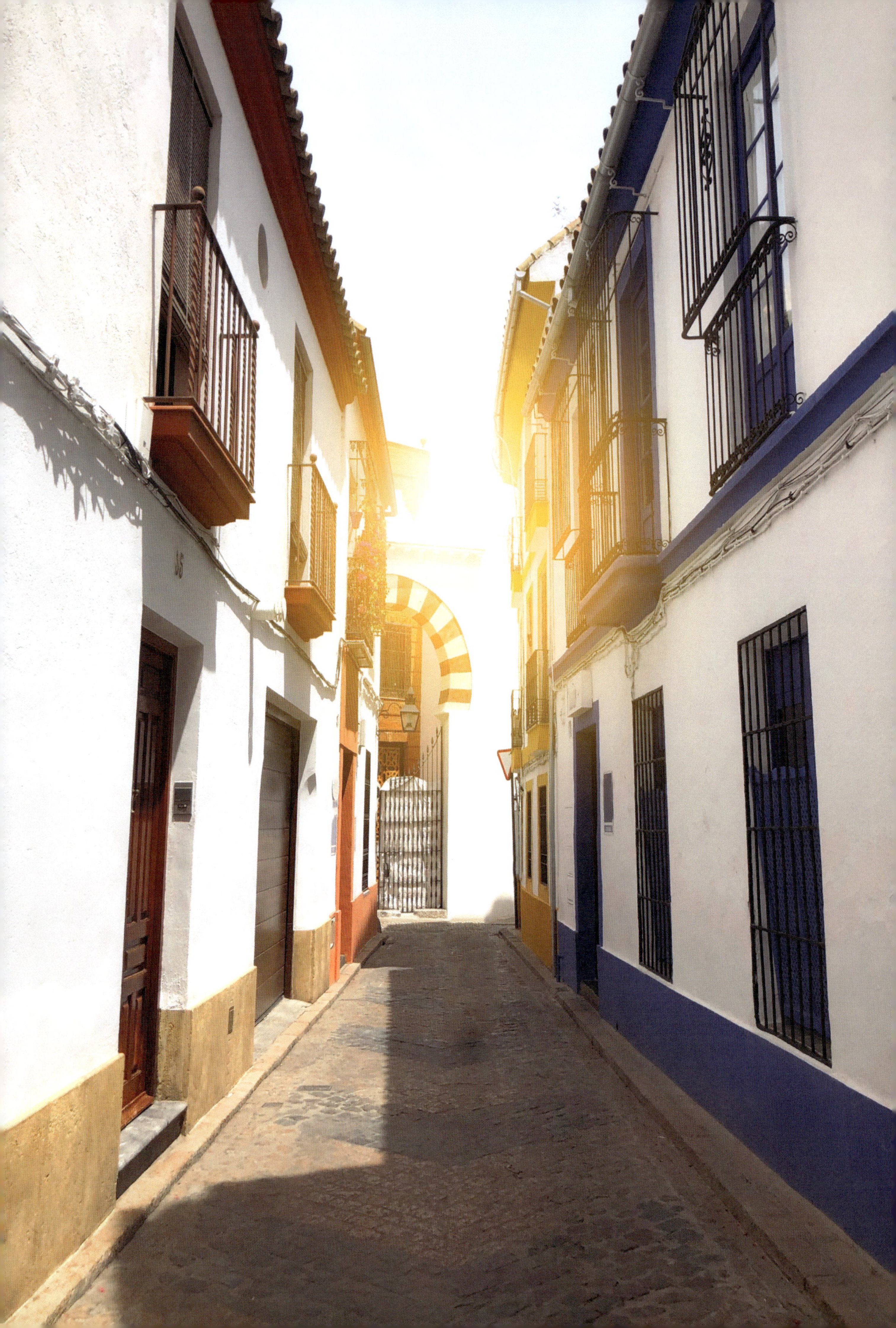

Spoon Dishes

COLD TOMATO SOUP Gazpacho

This recipe originally comes from Andalusia in Southern Spain. Nowadays it's the perfect starter to a summer meal even though Gazpacho was originally served at the end of a meal. Spaniards have it day in, day out during the hot summer period. It's very refreshing, easy to make, tasty and full of vitamins as it uses fresh vegetables.

SERVES 4:
650 gr. (1.4 lb.) good quality ripe red tomatoes
80 gr. (3 oz.) cucumber
50 gr. (1.7 oz.) green pepper
1 small garlic clove
1 thin slice of gluten-free bread
250 ml. (1 cup) ice water
½ tsp. wine vinegar
½ Tbsp. salt
4 Tbsp. Spanish extra Virgin olive oil
1 Tbsp. mayonnaise at room temperature (optional)

1. Cool the vegetables in the fridge for at least 1 hour before making the Gazpacho. Wash all the vegetables. Peel the garlic clove and remove its long core by cutting it lengthwise and then removing it with a knife (see photo on page 93).

2. Peel the cucumber and tomatoes. Pour the water into a blender. Add in all the ingredients chopped up into chunks. They may not fit at once, so you may have to blend them in batches. Blend until the mixture is smooth and pass through a sieve with a large bowl underneath it.

3. Always try it and adjust salt and vinegar to taste.

4. You can either drink it from an individual bowl or eat it with a spoon with sprinkled diced vegetables (cucumber, tomato, onion) and gluten-free croutons.

5. Serve immediately to take advantage of the vitamins. You could also refrigerate for 1 hour covered with cling film.

TIP: Some top chefs stir in 1 Tbsp. of mayonnaise after the ingredients have been blended.

SPOON DISHES

COLD CORDOVAN TOMATO AND BREAD CREME
Salmorejo

This dish originally comes from the Andalusian region of Córdoba. Along with Gazpacho, it is the most popular cold soup in Spain. In fact, many people find Salmorejo more delicious than its famous "cousin". It has influences from the Romans, Greeks and Arabs. It was created as a way to use up stale bread and at first didn't contain tomatoes. Its creaminess is derived from the way the oil and bread emulsify and then fuse with the tomatoes. In Córdoba, it is generally enjoyed by dipping bread or using a spoon.

SERVES 4:
1 kg. (23 oz.) good quality ripe red tomatoes
1 garlic clove
1 hardboiled yolk
150 gr. (5 oz.). gluten-free bread
½ Tbsp. salt
125 ml. (1/2 cup) Spanish extra Virgin olive oil
3 hardboiled eggs (optional)

1. Wash and peel the tomatoes. Circle the stem, then remove the core. Cut into quarters and place in a tall stand up food processor or blender.

2. Peel the garlic clove and remove its long core by cutting it lengthwise and then removing it with a knife (see photo on page 93). Add it into the blender.

3. Blend until the mixture is smooth. Add in the gluten-free bread and harboiled yolk. Season with salt. Blend again. While the blender is running, remove the lid and pour in little by little the olive oil. You should get an homogeneous smooth creme. If your blender is not big enough to do it in one go, do it in batches. Try and adjust salt. Refrigerate covered with cling film for at least 1 hour.

4. Meanwhile, hard-boil 3 eggs and once chilled, cut into small dices. Use as much as you want as garnish on top along with the diced eggs if you want.

SPOON DISHES

ALMOND AND GARLIC CRÈME Ajo Blanco

There is an ownership dispute between the Málaga and Granada regions of Andalusia over it origins, both claiming it. The term "Ajo Blanco" means "White Garlic" in Spanish and it refers to one of the main ingredients and the color of this dish. The old basic recipe didn't use any bread but the modern one includes it amongst its ingredients.

SERVES 4
150 gr. (5 oz.) stale crusty gluten-free bread guts
3 garlic cloves
100 gr. (3.5 oz.) skinless almonds
75 ml. (5 Tbsp.) Spanish extra virgin olive oil
1/2 Tbsp. white wine vinegar
salt to taste
For Decoration:
green grapes cut in half lengthwise melon slices (optional)
croutons (optional)

1. Cut the bread into chunks and soak them in water until tender. (Around 15-25 minutes depending on the type of bread).

2. Bring 1 liter (4 cups) of water to a boil and pour in the almonds. Stir well until it boils again and cook for 30 seconds. Take out the almonds with a strainer and place on kitchen roll to get rid of the water. Set the water aside. Let the almonds cool.

3. Put all the ingredients except the oil in a blender and add in 2 cups (500 ml.) of the water where you boiled the almonds. Blend for a minute until you get a smooth paste. While the blender is still on, take off the little lid and pour alternatively and little by little the olive oil and the remaining water set aside. Blend until you get a creamy soup.

4. Oil and water measures are approximate, so use as much as you need for a creamy soup consistency. Try and adjust salt to taste. Put in the fridge covered with cling film for at least 1 hour. Serve decorated with green grapes or melon.

LENTIL STEW Lentejas guisadas

This is a great dish full of hearty flavor. Spaniards eat it all year around. Simple, healthy, cheap and overall delicious. If you want to help your body absorb the high iron content of the lentils, accompany with a tomato salad or follow with some fruit rich in vitamin C.

SERVES 4
200 gr. (6.5 oz.) dry brown lentils
½ medium onion, finely chopped
½ green bell pepper, finely chopped
1 small tomato in chunks
2 carrots in slices
1 small potato

2 garlic cloves
1 bay leaf
2 Tbsp. Spanish extra Virgin olive oil
splash of white vinegar (optional)
a handful of rice (optional)
salt to taste

1. Heat 2 Tbsp. of oil in a large pot over a medium heat. Add in and fry the bay leaf, finely chopped garlic cloves, onion and green pepper until tender.

2. Add the lentils to the pot. Some lentils need soaking for an hour prior to cooking but others don't. It depends on the brand or type of lentils you buy. Check the seller's instructions.

3. Add 1.5 liters (6 cups) of cold water. Add the tomato. Bring to a boil over a high heat. When it starts boiling, pour in half a glass of cold water which will stop the boil. Bring again to a boil and stop it again with half a glass of cold water. Repeat a 3rd time. Put on a lid and simmer for 40 minutes.

4. Cut the carrots into 1/2 cm. (0.2 inch) thick slices. Cut the potato into 2.5 cm (1 inch) thick slices and stir them into the pot. Cook uncovered for 10 minutes. Add salt to taste now and not before, to tender up the lentils quicker.

5. Simmer for 40 minutes over medium-low heat and with the lid on. Add in the rice if using 30 minutes before finishing.

6. Before serving, adjust salt and make sure the lentils are tender. If they are a bit hard, cook longer. Some people like lentils with a splash of white vinegar added just before serving the dish.

LENT CHICKPEA STEW Potaje de Cuaresma

This is a very traditional Spanish Easter dish and it tastes better than you can imagine. There's nothing more typical than having this Potaje on Holy Friday and also on any Friday during "Cuaresma" Lent, the 40 days between Carnival and Easter. If you ever need to re-heat it in the pot, do it slowly so the chickpeas don't break.

SERVES 4
200 gr. (6.5 oz.) dried chickpeas
1 tsp. of baking soda
1 medium onion, finely chopped
2 peeled garlic cloves
200 gr. (6.5 oz.) fresh or frozen spinach
1 toast of gluten-free bread
1 medium potato
bay leaves
salt to taste
4 Tbsp. Spanish extra Virgin olive

1. Soak the chickpeas overnight in water with baking soda. Pour in enough water taking into account that the chickpeas will double in size. The next day, rinse the chickpeas under water and drain.

2. Fry the onion and bay leaves in a large pot with 2 Tbsp. olive oil over a medium heat until onion becomes tender.

3. Pour the chickpeas into the pot with 1.7 liters (7 cups) of warm water. Bring to a boil and reduce heat to low and simmer covering with a lid. Cook for 1h 30m. Add in the spinach.

4. Fry the garlic and gluten-free bread in a small frying pan with 2 Tbsp. of oil until golden. Transfer to a mortar and crush with a pestle until you get a paste or blend with a food processor with a drop of the water from the pot. Pour the mixture into the pot. Stir in and bring the chickpeas back to a low boil.

5. Peel and cut the potato into medium size chunks. Salt to taste and simmer for 50 minutes. Then, check if ingredients are tender. They might need more time depending on the hardness of the water or altitude. Also at the end, the water should reduce so that it barely covers the chickpeas.

WHITE BEAN STEW   Judías blancas guisadas

SERVES 4
200 gr. (6.5 oz.) dried white beans
1 tsp. of baking soda
1 bay leaf
1/2 medium onion, finely chopped
2 peeled garlic cloves, finely chopped
1/3 green bell pepper, finely chopped
1 small tomato in chunks
A splash of Spanish Virgin olive oil

1. Soak the white beans overnight in water with baking soda. Pour in enough water taking into account that the beans will double in size. The next day, rinse the beans under water and drain.

2. Add the beans to the pot. Pour enough water to just cover them.

3. Stir in the bay leaf and all the vegetables. Pour a splash of oil and season with salt to taste. Bring the water to a boil over a high heat.

4. When it starts boiling, pour in half a glass of cold water which will stop the boil. Bring again to a boil and stop it again with half a glass of cold water. Repeat a 3rd time. Put on a lid and simmer for 40 minutes or until the beans are tender. Try and adjust salt. Serve warm.

   TIP: You can use more ingredients such as spinach or cabbage.

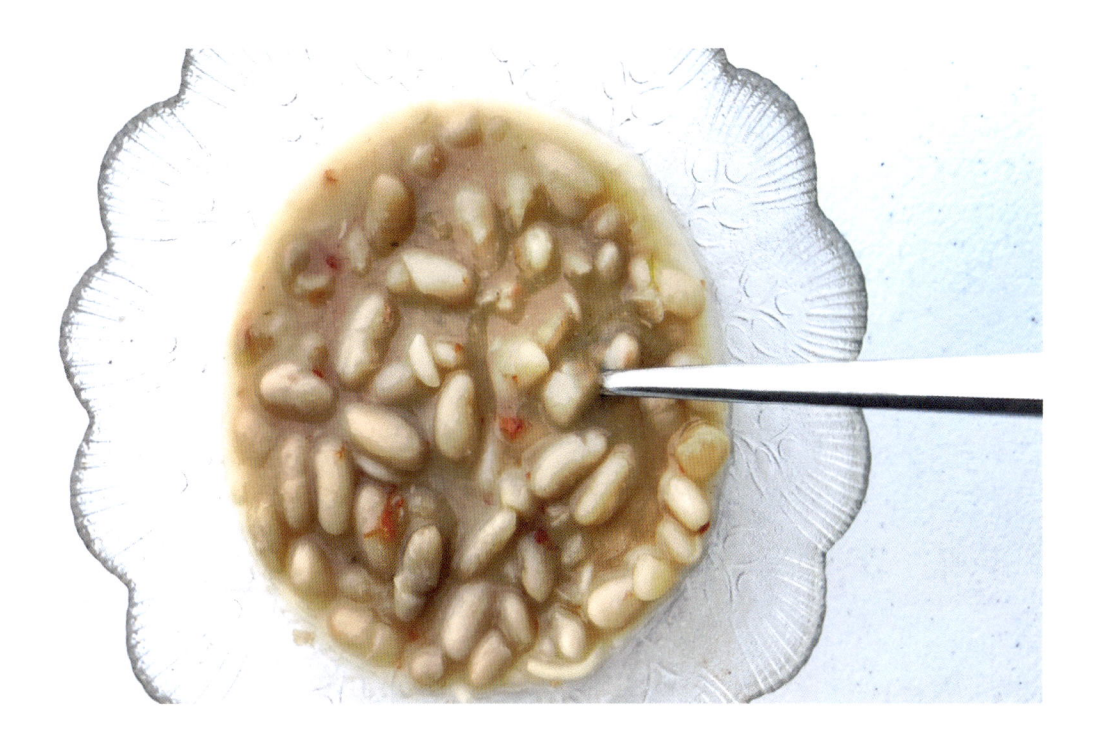

GARLIC SOUP CASTILLIAN STYLE
Sopa de ajo castellana

This is an ancient rural dish that originally comes from both the Castillian regions of Spain, which are "the land of bread". It's a very warming soup for cold Winter days.

SERVES 2
4 slices (1-1.5 cm/ 0.4-0.6 inches thick) of stale gluten-free bread
1 garlic clove, finely sliced
1 tsp. sweet paprika
600 ml. (2 ½ cup) warm water
1 bay leaf
salt to taste
ground black pepper to taste
Spanish extra Virgin olive oil

1. Fry 2 slices of bread in a small pan with 2 Tbsp. olive oil until golden on both sides and set aside.
2. Heat 2 Tbsp. olive oil in a casserole or pot and fry both sides of the other 2 bread slices along with the garlic. Fry over a medium heat for 2 minutes stirring occasionally.
3. Remove the casserole or pot from the heat and sprinkle the paprika on the bread. Stir and combine.
4. Pour in the warm water. Add a bay leaf. Simmer covered for 25 minutes.
5. Top the soup with the 2 gluten-free bread slices that you fried on step 1. Let them float and wait till they get soggy.
6. Try the soup and adjust salt and pepper to taste.

TIP: For more flavor and protein, you can break an egg into each bowl at the end of the preparation and bake it in the oven until the egg is set. You could also poach an egg in the soup itself for 3 minutes.

CREAMY MUSHROOM SOUP Crema champiñones

SERVES 2:
90 gr. (0.2 oz) leeks.
275 gr. (0.6 oz.) sliced mushrooms
300 ml. (1 1/4 cups) vegetable broth (page 92) or water
1 Tbsp. cream cheese at room temperature
Spanish Virgin olive oil
salt to taste

1. Wash and press the mushrooms in your hand so the water in them comes out. Cut off their tails. Slice them finely.

2. Heat 3-4 Tbsp. of oil in a large pot over a medium heat. Add in and fry the mushrooms and leeks covered with a lid over until tender. Stir occasionally. Take out and reserve 4 slices of mushroom to decorate at the end

3. Pour in the vegetable broth. Bring to a boil. Season with salt. Lower the heat and simmer over a medium-low heat with a lid for about 20 minutes or until all vegetables are tender. Remove from the heat and stir in the cream cheese.

4. Blend with a hand blender. Oil and broth/ water measures are approximate, so use as much as you need for a creamy soup consistency. Try and adjust salt to taste. Decorate with some fried mushroom slices on top. Serve immediately.

CREAMY ZUCCHINI SOUP Crema de calabacín

SERVES 4:
600 gr. (1.4 oz.) zucchini in small cubes
1 medium onion, finely chopped
1 medium potato, peeled and in small cubes
250 ml. (1 cup) vegetable broth (page 92) or warm water
100 ml. (3/4 cup) cream/milk/soy cream
Spanish extra Virgin olive oil
salt to taste
ground black pepper to taste
fresh parsley/ flaxseeds/pumpkin seeds for decoration(optional)

1. Heat 4 Tbsp. of oil in a pot or saucepan over a medium heat. Stir in and fry the finely chopped onion and potato in cubes for 5 minutes. Stir in the zucchini. Season with salt and fry for another 5 minutes.

2. Pour the vegetable broth or warm water into the saucepan. Bring to a boil. Lower the heat and simmer over a medium-low heat with a lid for about 20 minutes or until all vegetables are tender. Remove from the heat and stir in the cream.

3. Blend with a hand blender. Oil and water/broth measures are approximate, so use as much as you need for a creamy soup consistency. Try and adjust salt to taste. Serve immediately.

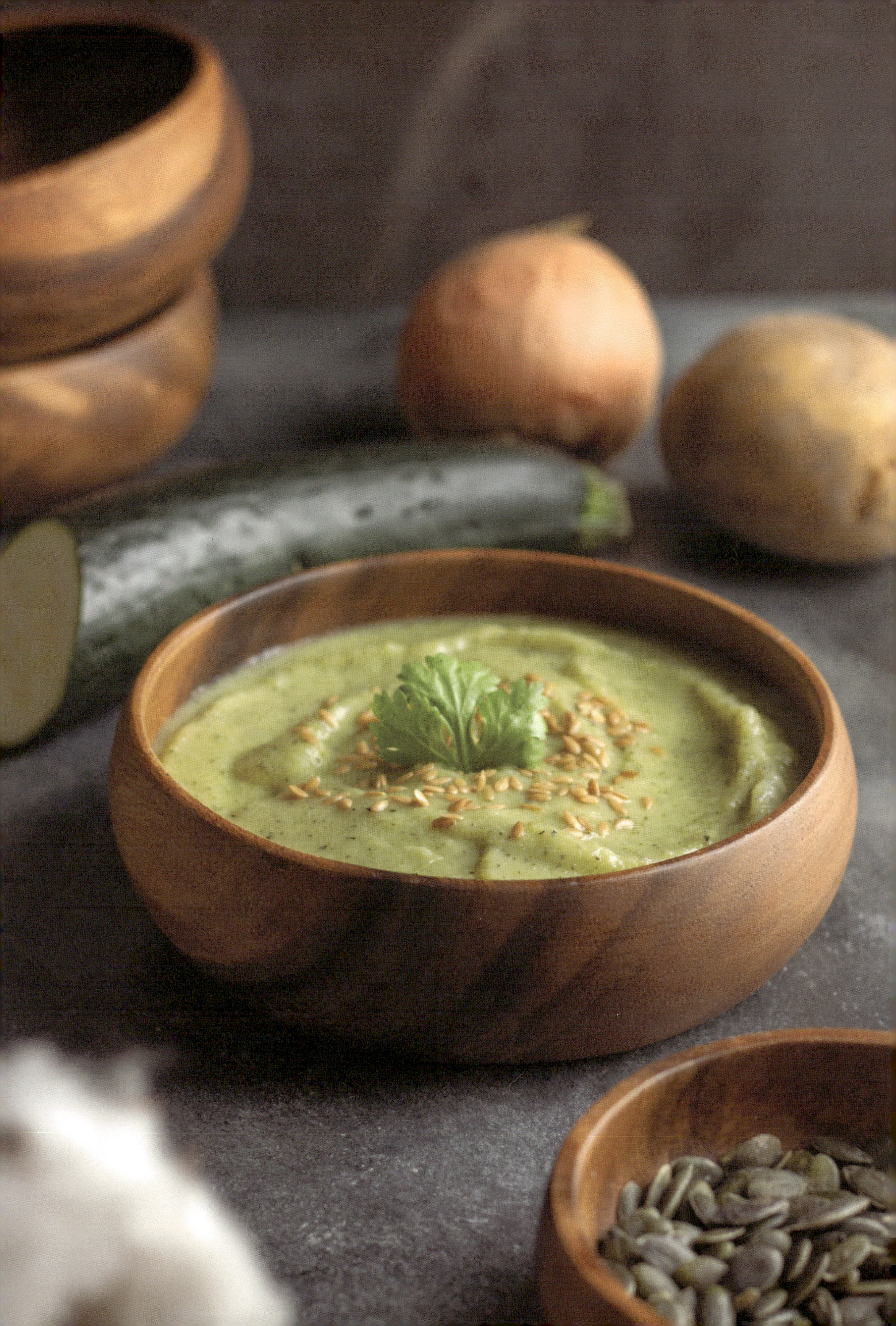

LEEK SOUP Porrusalda

The term Porrusalda comes from the Basque words "porru" for leek and "salda" for broth. In the olden days, it used to be a Lent dish and is believed to have humble origins.

SERVES 4-6
1 medium size onion
6 leeks
400 gr. (14 oz.). potatoes
1.2 liters (5 cups) water
salt to taste
ground black pepper to taste
2 Tbsp. Spanish extra Virgin olive oil
2 large carrots (160 gr./5 oz.)

1. Peel and finely chop the onion. Fry in a wide pot with 2 Tbsp. of olive oil over a medium-low heat. When the onion is tender and before it gets golden, pour in the water.

2. Wash the leeks and cut into slices. Then cut them in half. Fold them into the soup. Wash the potatoes and carrots.

3. Cut the potatoes into irregular chunks about 2.5 cm. (1 inch) wide and the carrots into medium thick slices. Mix them into the pot. Add salt and pepper to taste. Simmer covered with a lid for 18-20 minutes. Serve warm.

Pasta & Rice

CLAY DISH Greixonera

The name of this dish comes from the Majorcan word for the clay dish in which it is served. A very unusual recipe as it is a savory dish with cinnamon. Nevertheless, you'll see how well the cinnamon brings out the flavors of the other ingredients.

SERVES 4
350 gr. (12 oz.) any gluten-free penne or pasta of your choice
150 gr. (5.2 oz.) grated Mahon cheese or Emmental if you can't find it
100 gr. (3.5 oz.) butter/margarine
250 ml. (1 cup) milk
1 tsp. ground cinnamon
4 hardboiled eggs (optional)
salt to taste

1. Pre-heat oven to 220°C (425°F).
2. Bring a large pot of salted water to a boil. Add the pasta and boil according to package instructions. When done, drain off the water and set pasta aside.
3. Warm up the milk in a pot, add in the pasta and simmer until the milk reduces.
4. Sprinkle ¾ of the cheese, ¾ tsp cinnamon and a 1 tsp. of salt. Combine well with a spoon. Pour the pasta into a large clay dish or small individual clay dishes. You can also use any other type of oven dish.
5. Top with the remaining cheese and ¼ tsp. of cinnamon.
6. Hard boil the eggs if using.
7. Place the hardboiled eggs, peeled and in quarters on top. Top every egg with a bit of butter and then spread the remaining butter in small chunks on top of the pasta.
8. Grill in the pre-heated oven for 10 minutes until cheese is light golden brown. Serve immediately.

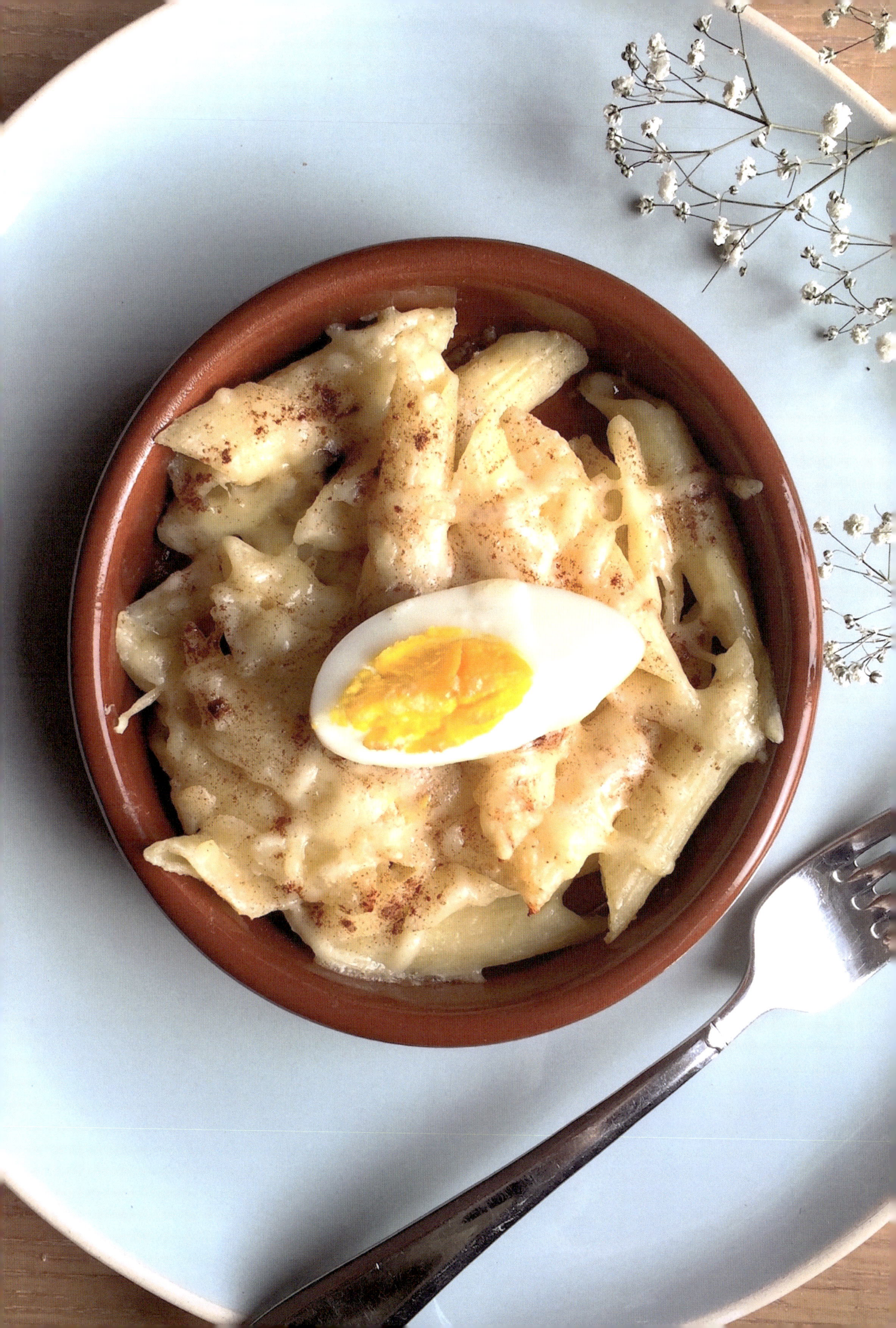

PASTA GARLIC STYLE Pasta al ajillo

SERVES 4
350 gr. (12 oz.) any gluten-free spaghetti or pasta of your choice
3 large garlic cloves, finely minced
4 Tbsp. Spanish extra Virgin olive oil
1 dried cayenne pepper (optional)
Freshly minced parsley (optional)

1. Bring a large pot of salted water to a boil. Add the pasta and boil according to package instructions. When done, drain off the water and set pasta aside.

2. Heat 4 Tbsp. of olive oil in a non-stick frying pan over a medium heat. Fry the cayenne pepper and garlic cloves until light golden. Be careful because they can burn really quickly.

3. Stir in the pasta. Mix well and for cook about 3 minutes stirring occasionally.

4. Sprinkle chopped parsley on top.

PENNE WITH FUNGHI AND CHEESE
Macarrones al queso con setas

This is a traditional dish from the Catalonia Region. It was usually made with "moixernós" mushrooms, but nowadays it can be found with any type of funghi.

SERVES 4
350 gr. (12 oz.) any gluten-free penne or pasta of your choice
300 gr. (10.5 oz.) any type of funghi
4 ripe tomatoes
1 medium onion, finely minced
Salt to taste
A pinch of ground nutmeg
100 gr. (3.5 oz.) grated cheese
Spanish Virgin olive oil

1. Bring a large pot of salted water to a boil. Add the pasta and boil according to package instructions. When done, drain off the water and set pasta aside.

2. Wash the funghi with water and then press them in your hands to get rid of the excess water. Cut them into thin slices. Peel, deseed and grind the tomatoes.

3. Heat up 3 lugs of oil in a casserole. When the oil is hot, fry the onion over a medium heat until translucent. Stir in the tomato. Fry stirring frequently until both are tender.

4. Add in the sliced funghi and fry for 3 minutes stirring frequently. Pour in some water if gets too dry. Season with salt. Stir in the pasta and season with nutmeg. Mix well and cook about 3 minutes stirring occasionally. Sprinkle with grated cheese and grill in oven until cheese is golden.

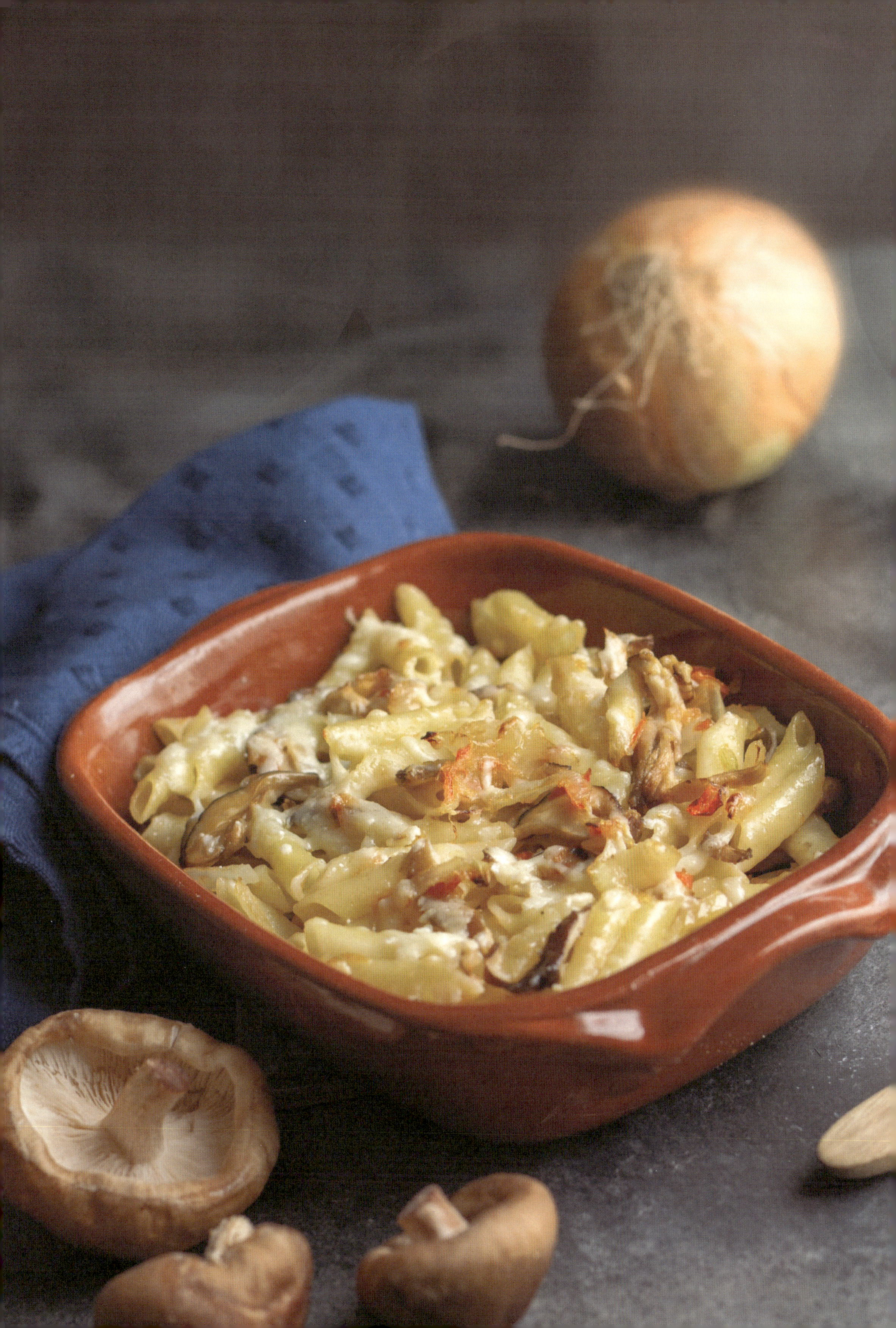

VEGETABLE PAELLA Paella de verduras

This is no ordinary vegetable rice. The technic followed by this recipe is the same as the one followed by the Original Valencian Paella recipe except no animal protein has been used. This dish is so full of flavor that is astonishingly similar to the original.

SERVES 4-5
200 gr. (7 oz.) bomb or round rice
8 large artichokes
100 gr. (3.5 oz.). flat green beans
3 garlic cloves
½ green bell pepper
12 lima beans ("garrofó" beans)
1 small peeled tomato
700 ml. (3 cups) vegetable broth (see page 92)
6-7 saffron threads
salt to taste
Spanish extra Virgin olive oil
Rosemary for decoration

1. Use a paella pan (paellera) which is a large flat open round pan with handles or a large electric skillet or pan with a base at least 40 cm (15-16 inches) wide. The key for a proper Paella is cooking the rice evenly spread in a thin layer all round the pan in order to absorb all the flavors from the other ingredients. That's why a wide pan is a must.
2. Clean artichokes following method in step 1 of the recipe VEGETABLE STEW NAVARRAN STYLE on page 16. Finely chop the green pepper.
3. Heat 4 lugs of oil in the paellera. Fry the artichokes and green pepper over a medium heat. When they're almost done (soft), stir in the finely chopped garlic cloves and flat green beans.
4. Cut the tomato into small chunks and stir into the pan. Sprinkle the sweet paprika.
5. Add in the lima beans. Season with salt to taste and mix well. This mixture is called "sofrito". Gently cook the mixture for 10 minutes with the lid on, stirring frequently.
6. Add the rice to the paellera and cook for 5-7 minutes over a medium-low heat, stirring constantly.
7. Pour in the vegetable broth. You can buy the broth already made or prepare it yourself. To make vegetable broth, follow the recipe on page 92.
8. Put the saffron threads into a mortar and crush them into dust. Pour 1 Tbsp. of broth from the Paella into the mortar. Mix it with the saffron dust and stir well. Pour the resulting orange liquid into the paellera.
9. Cover with a lid and lower to medium-low heat so it reduces to a gentle boil. From now on, don't disturb or stir the rice. Move the paellera around as much as you want to even out the heat, but <u>don't stir the rice</u>. Check the liquid from time to time and add more water if the rice looks dry. It will take 15-20 minutes in total to fully cook. If the paellera has been set over two burners or heat rings, cover it with foil for the last 2 minutes of cooking to ensure the rice cooks evenly.
10. The rice should be dry and separate easily when done, not creamy like risotto. Once cooked, remove the Paella from the heat. If the rice is still a bit hard, you can cover the paellera with a damp cloth and let it rest for 10 min. If it's fully cooked, let it rest uncovered. You can also place the paellera uncovered in a heated oven at 425°F (215°C) for the last 10 minutes of cooking.
11. The crunchy crust of rice that sticks to the bottom of the paellera is the "reward" from a well-made Paella and is called the "Socarrat".

PASTA & RICE

POTATOES WITH RICE Patatas con arroz

This recipe is not very well known abroad. Here I'll let you in on a secret that a few Spaniards know about. It's unusual because it's a rice recipe eaten with a spoon.

SERVES 4 -6
300 gr. (1 1/2 cup) round rice
750 gr. (1.5 lb.) potatoes
2 garlic cloves
½ tsp. sweet paprika
1 bay leaf
1 ½ liter (6 cups) aprox. water
salt to taste
Spanish Extra Virgin olive oil

1. Fry one finely minced garlic clove in a pan with 2 Tbsp. of olive oil over a medium heat until light golden. Remove the pan from the heat and sprinkle the sweet paprika over the pan. Set aside.

2. Peel the potatoes and cut into middle size chunks. You can choose not to peel them if the potatoes are bio. Place the potato chunks in a large saucepan. Pour the water into the saucepan and season with salt. Stir in 1 crushed garlic clove and 1 bay leaf in the water. Pour in the contents of the frying pan. Bring to a boil over a high heat. Lower the heat and simmer covered over a medium-low heat for 10 minutes. Add in the rice and simmer for 15-20 minutes. Try and adjust salt. Let it rest for 5 minutes. The rice shouldn't be dry. It should have a soupy consistency. If the water seems to be evaporating too quickly while you are cooking the rice, then add a drop more.

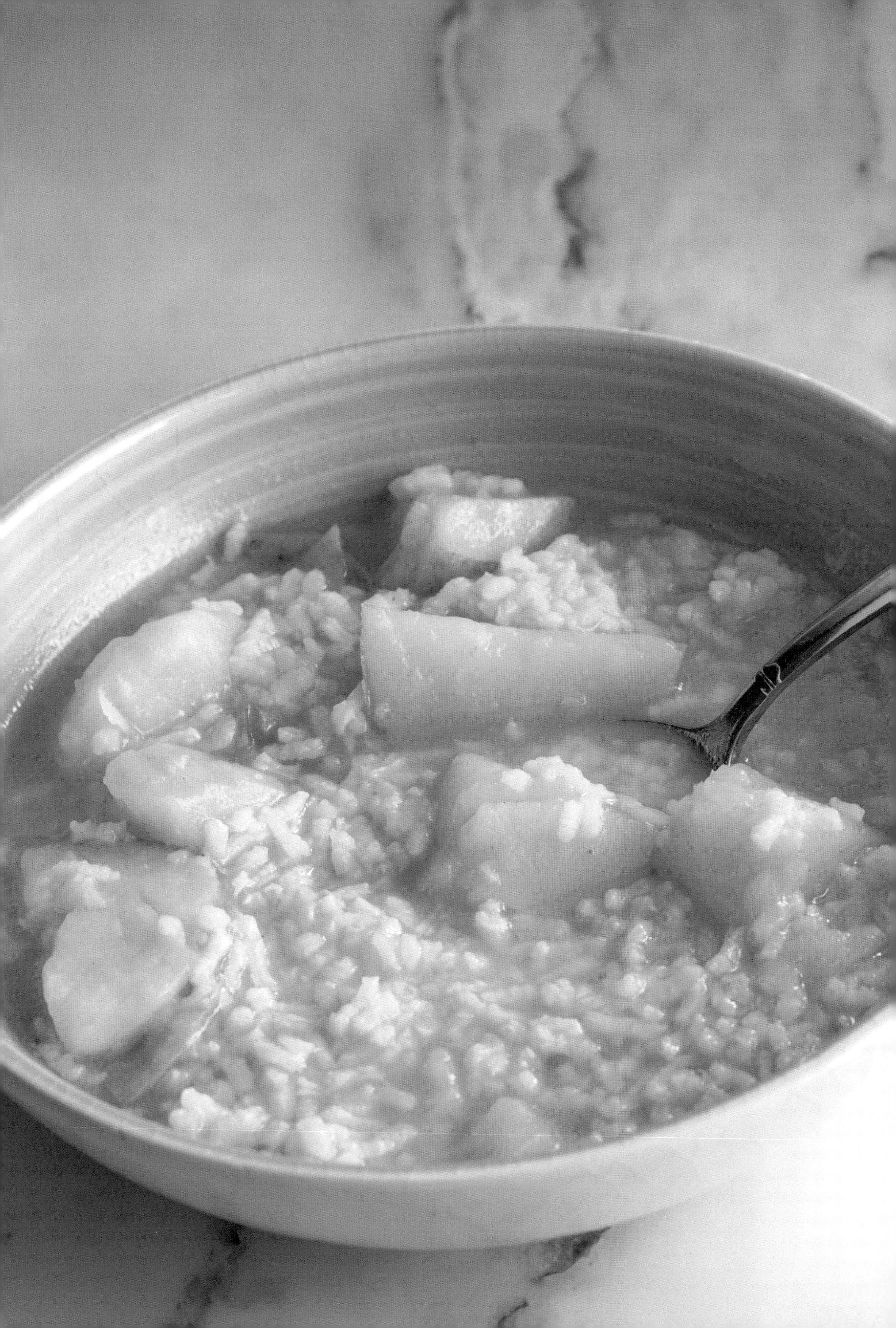

PASTA & RICE

CUBAN STYLE RICE Arroz a la Cubana

Despite the name, this is a traditional dish in Spain's gastronomy, especially in the Canary Islands. It was created by the Spanish "emigrés" in South and Central America during colonial times. The popular Latin-American version has a fried banana in it, but it didn't really catch on in Spain.

SERVES 1: *1 egg - 50 gr. (1.7 oz.) rice - 30 ml. (2 Tbsp.) fried tomato puree - olive oil – salt to taste – fresh parsley*

1. Boil the rice according to the manufacturer's instructions. Drain and set aside.

2. Crack one egg onto a plate and season with salt.

3. Heat up 2 Tbsp. olive oil in a small pan over a medium-high heat. Carefully slip the egg into the oil and immediately turn the heat down to low. Fry until edges of the egg whites are golden. Tilt the frying pan and pour oil from the pan over the egg with a ladle or spoon, in order to also fry the top. But don't pour hot olive oil over the egg yolk if you like a runny yolk

4. Warm up the fried tomato puree in the microwave with a lid on for 15 seconds or in a pot over a low heat.

5. Place the fried egg with the boiled rice on a plate. Pour the tomato puree all over the rice and decorate with parsley.

Eggs

SPANISH POTATO OMELETTE Tortilla de Patata

This is one of the most famous Spanish recipes. The one here includes onions but you could also make it without. There are many variations which contain different ingredients, like sliced chorizo, ham, zucchini, peppers, etc.

MAKES 1 LARGE OMELETTE FOR 3-4 PEOPLE: 5 large beaten eggs – 3 medium potatoes - 1 medium onion - Spanish olive oil - salt to taste

1. Wash the potatoes under running water. Peel them and <u>do not wash</u> them again. Cut into thin half slices.
2. Peel, wash and finely chop the onion. Use a 23 cm. (9 inch) based pan. Heat 3-4 lugs of olive oil over a medium heat. Wait until the oil is hot and then carefully add the potatoes and onion. The oil should at least cover the bottom half of the potatoes. Season with salt. Cover with a lid and fry over medium-low heat while stirring occasionally.
3. After 7 minutes, break the potatoes with a wooden spatula in the pan. Stir well and cover. Fry until completely done (around 20 min.). Take out the potato and onion mixture with a slotted spoon or ladle and place in a sieve with a bowl underneath so the oil drips into it.
4. Place eggs in a large bowl and add 2 pinches of salt. Beat by hand and add the potato onion mixture. Combine.
5. You will cook the omelette in a smaller and non-stick 20 cm. (8 inch) based pan. You could also use an even smaller pan to make a smaller but thicker omelette. Pour 1 Tbsp. of the remaining olive oil from the bowl into the pan and heat over a medium heat. When the oil is hot, but before smoking hot, pour the potato-egg mixture into the pan. Spread out evenly. Move the pan around. If some parts of the omelette don't move, this means it has stuck to the pan. Using a non-stick spatula, scrape underneath the bottom. Cover the frying pan with a lid and allow the omelette to cook around the edges over a <u>low heat</u> (about 8 min. depending on the size of the pan).
6. Find a plate which is larger than the pan and place it upside down over the pan. Hold the handle with one hand and the top of the plate with the other.
7. Quickly flip the pan over and the omelette will "fall" onto the plate. Place the pan back on the heat and pour a quick splash of olive oil into the pan.
8. Carefully slide the omelette into the frying pan. Use the spatula to flatten the sides of the omelette. Let it cook covered over a low heat for 5-6 minutes. Turn the heat off and let it sit in the pan for 2 minutes.
9. Slide the omelette onto a large plate to serve. It can be a main course or a tapa.

ALSO A TAPA

BROKEN EGGS Huevos Rotos

This is a dish you'll find in any Spanish restaurant. Spaniards usually eat this for lunch or dinner but never for breakfast. When non-Spaniards try it, they are impressed and it usually becomes one of their favorite Spanish dishes. The original version only has potatoes and eggs. It may sound boring but it's amazingly delicious when properly made.

SERVES 2
4 eggs
700 gr. (1.5 lb.) potatoes
Spanish extra Virgin olive oil
salt to taste

1. Wash the potatoes and cut into slices. Wash again under running water to get rid of the starch. Heat up olive oil in a large frying pan. The oil should at least cover the bottom half of the potato slices. Place them into the hot oil and fry over a medium heat, stirring frequently. Add salt to taste. Remove with a slotted spoon when they turn light golden brown, after about 12 minutes. Set aside to cool on a paper towel lined plate. You could also bake the potato slices in the oven. Just pour olive oil over the potato slices and season with salt. Bake at 190°C (375 °F) until golden and tender (about 20-30 minutes).
2. Crack one egg onto a plate and season with salt.
3. Pour the left over oil used to fry the potato slices, into a small non-stick frying pan. There should be a good amount of oil (1 finger deep). Heat it over a medium-high heat until it begins to smoke.
4. Carefully slip the egg into the oil and immediately turn the heat down to low. Fry until edges of the egg white are golden. Tilt the frying pan and pour oil from the pan over the egg with a ladle or spoon, in order to also fry the top. Nevertheless, don't pour hot olive oil over the egg yolk if you like it runny. Repeat again for every egg.
5. Place the potato slices on a plate or small paellera. Using a slotted spoon, lift out the eggs and transfer on top of the potatoes. Break the eggs using 2 spoons and serve immediately.

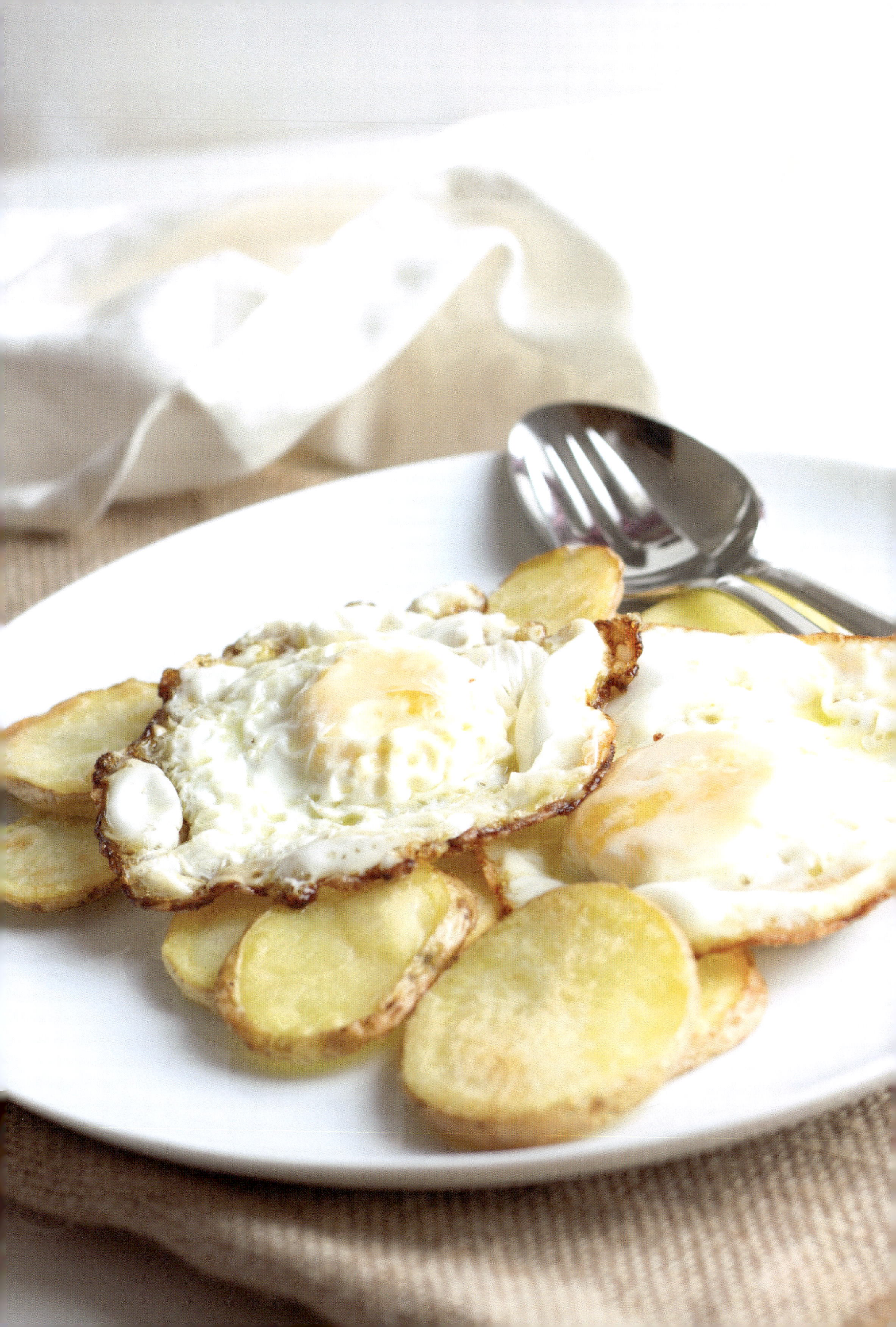

CARLISTAS EGGS Huevos Carlistas

The origin of both the name and the recipe is a mystery, but what we know for sure is that they are delicious. The classic version uses fried eggs but you could also use hardboiled ones. (they are easier to handle).

FOR 4 EGGS
4 eggs
salt to taste

For the batter:
4 Tbsp. Buckwheat flour
4 Tbsp. Chickpea flour
2 beaten eggs
4 Tbsp. gluten-free breadcrumbs
salt and pepper
Spanish extra virgin olive oil

For the Bechamel:
80 gr (2.8 oz.) butter
60 gr (2.1 oz.) corn flour
10 gr buckwheat flour
10 gr. chickpea flour
500 ml (2 cups) lactose free milk
salt to taste
ground black pepper to taste

1. Hard boil the eggs and peel them. Let them cool.
2. Prepare the thick bechamel with the quantities indicated on this recipe following the Thick bechamel recipe on page 94. Set aside and refrigerate for 1 hour.
3. Take the bechamel out of the fridge. Knead the bechamel with your hands so it has some elasticity back and you can work with it.
4. Place a handful of cool thick bechamel on one hand and then place the hardboiled egg in the middle. Cover the egg using another handful of bechamel with the other hand. Press the bechamel with your hands against the egg. Cover the egg completely and set aside. Repeat process for every egg.
5. Prepare 3 plates: one with the mixed gluten-free flour, another with 2 beaten eggs and the last one with gluten-free breadcrumbs.
6. Roll each egg in the flour, shaking off any excess.
7. Press each egg on the plate with the beaten eggs and dip it. With a fork, roll them so they are completely coated by the egg.
8. Lift it out of the beaten egg and roll in the bread crumbs coating each egg evenly.
9. Heat up a good amount of olive oil in a frying pan over a high-medium heat. The amount of oil depends on the size of the pan. The oil must cover the bottom half of the eggs and be quite hot at first. When it's hot (but before getting smoky hot) place them carefully in the oil. Lower the heat to a medium heat. Fry them in small batches. Turn them gently, for about 2 minutes, or until they are golden on all sides.
10. Using a slotted spoon, lift out the eggs, holding them briefly over the pan to allow excess oil to drain, and transfer to a paper towel lined plate to drain further. Serve warm.

ALSO A TAPA

OPENED EGGS WITH GREEN ASPARAGUS

Huevos abiertos con espárragos verdes

Typical egg recipe from the Aragonese region. Some versions use white instead of green asparagus and add cured ham.

SERVES 4:
4 eggs
3 garlic cloves, finely minced
100 gr. (3.5 oz.) green asparagus
2 Tbsp. any gluten-free flour of your choice
50 ml. (3 Tbsp). extra Virgin olive oil
500 ml (2 cups) vegetable broth (page 92) or water
ground parsley and salt

1. Pour the oil in a XL pan and heat over a medium heat. When hot, fry the garlic until light golden.

2. Add the gluten-free flour and fry for 1 minute.

3. Pour the water or broth and bring to a boil. Use a carrot peeler to take off the outer layer of the asparagus. Stir them and the rice into the boiling broth. As soon as you stir them in, the boiling will stop. Keep the heat high and wait for a second boil.

4. Season with salt. Lower the heat to medium-low and cover with a lid. Simmer for 15 minutes.

5. Crack the eggs one by one onto a plate. Gently slide in one egg at a time. Sprinkle salt over the eggs. Use a spoon to push some of the egg whites closer to their yolks. Cover and simmer for 10 minutes. Sprinkle parsley on top and serve.

SCRAMBLED EGGS WITH ASPARAGUS AND FUNGHI
Revuelto de esparragos y setas

Spaniards have a way with eggs. They love them scrambled but they will rarely have them for breakfast. This dish is very simple and easy to prepare but it is served in Spanish homes at lunch, dinner or as a tapa.

SERVES 4
8 large eggs, beaten
400 gr. (14 oz.) funghi or any type of mushrooms
200 gr. (7 oz.) green fresh very thin asparagus with the woody part off
2 large garlic cloves, minced
2 Tbsp. Spanish extra Virgin olive oil
salt to taste
fresh parsley
ground black pepper

1. Cut off the woody part at the bottom of each stalk of the green asparagus. Use a carrot peeler to take off their outer layer if they are not very thin. Also, they have to be previously blanched in boiling salted water for 2 minutes if the asparagus are not very thin. Set aside.

2. Cut the asparagus into large chunks. Slice the funghi/mushrooms and finely mince the garlic cloves.

3. Heat 2-3 Tbsp. of olive oil over a medium heat in a frying pan. Fry the green asparagus chunks for 2 minutes. Add in the funghi and garlic. Stir occassionally. Cook for about 3-5 minutes or until ingredients are cooked.

4. Whisk the eggs by hand in a bowl for 1 minute. Season with salt. Pour the eggs all over the ingredients in the pan and stir with a wooden spoon or spatula. Cook for 1 minute stirring constantly over low heat.

5. Sprinkle with black pepper and parsley.

ALSO A TAPA

GIRALDA EGGS Huevos a la Giralda

This recipe is named after the "Giralda" bell tower of the Seville Cathedral, whose construction was finished in 1189. This Andalusian recipe can be modified by changing the vegetables to suit your taste.

SERVES 4
4 eggs
2 medium onions, finely chopped
4 medium tomatoes, peeled and finely chopped
2 small green bell peppers, finely chopped
2 small red bell peppers, finely chopped
3 garlic cloves, finely minced
a splash of any white vinegar
salt to taste
½ Tbsp. sugar
1 ½ Tbsp. Spanish extra Virgin olive oil

1. Fry the onions, peppers and garlic until tender in a deep-frying pan with oil over a medium-low heat.
2. Add the tomatoes, sugar and salt to taste. Combine well and simmer with a lid on for 15 minutes over a low heat.
3. To poach the eggs, heat 5 cm. (2 inches) of water in a small pot over a medium-high heat. Pour a splash of vinegar. Crack one egg into a plate and slide it into the boiling water. If the yolk brakes, then discard it. Repeat with the remaining eggs. Leave room between the eggs, preparing in two, three or single batches if need be. Cook eggs, undisturbed, until white is just set and yolk is still runny, approx. 3 to 4 minutes. Gently use a spatula to release eggs from the bottom of the pan, if necessary.
4. Using a slotted spoon, remove each egg from water and transfer to individual dishes. Cover each egg with the vegetables from the pan and serve.

Tapas

MUSHROOM GARLIC STYLE Champiñones al ajillo

This is a very typical "pincho" in the Basque Country. It usually served on a slice of crusty bread.

SERVES 4:
8 large mushrooms
salt to taste
2 garlic cloves
Spanish extra Virgin olive oil
Fresh parsley

1. Peel the garlic cloves and crush in a mortar. Add the parsley and a pinch of salt. Continue crushing until you get a homogeneous paste. Pour 50 ml. (3 Tbsp). of olive oil slowly while stirring the paste with the pestle. If you don't have a mortar, you can use a blender. Set aside.

2. Clean the mushrooms with a wet vegetable brush. Remove their tails with your hands and reserve for another recipe. Place the mushroom heads in a bowl and pour in about 2 Tbsp. olive oil so they get coated in the oil. Season with salt. Mix well with your hands.

3. Fry the mushroom heads up in a pan with a splash olive oil for 2-3 minutes or until you see golden edges.

4. Turn them over and spoon the garlic-parsley sauce into the hole left in the mushroom head by the removal of the tail. Cook for 3 minutes until cooked. Serve immediately.

5. You can have them as is or in pairs on top of toasted gluten-free crusty bread with an inserted toothpick all the way through to keep all ingredients together

STUFFED MUSHROOMS WITH SPINACH AND PINENUTS
Champiñones rellenos de espinacas y piñones

MAKES 4 MUSHROOMS:
4 large mushrooms
1 garlic clove, finely minced
150 gr. (5 oz.) fresh spinach
A bunch of pine nuts
1/2 Tbsp. Dijon mustard
1 tsp. honey/agave
Salt to taste
Spanish extra Virgin olive oil

1. Follow steps 2 and 3 of previous recipe.

2. Turn them over and fry until fully cooked. You can add some more oil the mushrooms get too dry. Place in an oven tray.

3. Heat 3 Tbsp. olive oil and fry the spinach and the garlic stirring constantly. When the spinach has reduced considerably in size, mix in the mustard and honey/agave and cook for 1-2 minutes, stirring well. Season with salt. Spoon the content of the pan into the mushrooms.

4. Place the pine nuts on top of the spinach and grill in oven at 180-190 °C (356-375 °F) until pine nuts are golden.

5. Serve immediately.

TOMATO TOAST Pan con tomate

This is a recipe from the Catalan region and there it is called "Pa amb tomàquet". You can also find it in Mallorca, Valencia and Aragon regions. People have it as an everyday tapa but mainly as a very typical ordinary breakfast. It can also be served with grilled vegetables, escalivada (page 10) and cheese. Fortunately, nowadays, you can find very nice gluten-free crusty bread so you can enjoy this simple but incredible recipe.

SERVES 1
1 ripe tomato
2 slices of gluten-free crusty bread
1 garlic clove
Salt to taste
a drizzle of Spanish extra Virgin olive oil

1. Cut two slices of gluten-free crusty bread and fry both sides with a splash of olive oil in a pan. You can also toast in a toaster.

2. Cut the garlic clove lengthwise in half. Rub each half on the toasts.

3. Wash a ripe tomato and cut it in half. Rub each half tomato on the toasts.

4. Sprinkle with salt.

5. Drizzle with Spanish extra Virgin olive oil.

ZUCCHINI & MUSHROOM TOAST
Tosta de calabacín y champiñón

MAKES 4 TOASTS
1 medium zucchini/courgetti
4 toasts of gluten-free bread
4 large mushrooms
Spanish extra Virgin olive oil
4 Tbsp. grated cheese of your choice
salt to taste
a pinch of ground black pepper
ground parsley to taste

1. Wash and slice the zucchini/courgette. Fry in a pan with oil until tender. Remove and set aside.
2. Wash and press the mushrooms in your hand so the water in them comes out. Cut off their tails. Slice them up. Fry in a pan with oil and season with salt and pepper. Cook until tender.
3. To assemble, place each toast on a tray. Top them with the fried zucchini and mushrooms on top. Sprinkle grated cheese. Grill in oven till golden.
4. Take out of the oven. Sprinkle freshly ground parsley and enjoy.

MUSHROOM & BECHAMEL TOAST
Tosta de champiñones y bechamel

MAKES 4 TOASTS
4 large mushrooms
1 garlic clove
crusty gluten-free bread
salt to taste
ground black pepper to taste
4 handfuls of grated cheese

For the bechamel:
80 gr (2.8 oz.) butter/margarine
60 gr (2.1 oz.) corn flour
5 gr buckwheat flour
5 gr. chickpea flour
600 ml (2 ½ cups) lactose free milk/soy milk
salt to taste
ground black pepper to taste

1. Wash and press the mushrooms in your hand so the water in them comes out. Cut off their tails. Slice them up. Fry in a pan with oil along with the garlic cloves. Season with salt and pepper. Cook until tender and set aside.
2. Prepare the bechamel following recipe in page 94
3. Add in the mushrooms and garlic into the bechamel and mix well.
4. Spoon on top of the bread.
5. Sprinkle a handful of grated cheese on top. Grill in the oven until cheese is golden.

GOAT CHEESE AND TOMATO JAM TAPA
Montadito de queso de cabra con mermelada de tomate

MAKES 1 TOAST
1 Crusty gluten-free slice of bread
2-3 slices of goat cheese
½ Tbsp. tomato jam

1. Cut one slice of gluten-free crusty bread. Top it with the goat cheese slices. Grill in the oven until golden.

2. Take out of the oven. Lift the cheese with a metal spatula. Spread some tomato jam on the bread and place the cheese goat back on top of the jam.

GOAT CHEESE & CARAMELIZED ONION TAPA
Montadito de queso de cabra con cebolla caramelizada

MAKES 4 TOASTS
4 Crusty gluten-free slices of bread
12 slices of goat cheese
1 large onion
Spanish olive oil
a splash of balsamic vinegar (optional)
a handful of chopped walnuts

1. Heat 2 Tbsp. olive oil in a non-stick frying pan and when hot, stir in the onion cut into thin strips. Cook over high-medium heat, stirring constantly.

2. When the onions is light brown, lower the heat. Season with salt and simmer with a lid on between 30 minutes to 1 hour. Try not to stir the onion for the first 20 minutes. You can add some more oil or water if the get too dry. After that time, stir every few minutes. If the onion gets too dry, add some water until fully cooked and browned.

3. At the end of the process, some balsamic vinegar can be added to deglaze the pan and bring some additional flavor. Set aside.

4. Slice the gluten-free crusty bread. Top the slices with the goat cheese. Grill in the oven or fry in a pan until golden.

5. Take out of the oven. Top with the caramelized onion and decorate with chopped walnuts

BRAVE POTATOES Patatas Bravas

This recipe has many versions with different sauces. The one I am going to show you here is very typical in the city of Zaragoza in Aragón and to my taste, is the best one.

SERVES 6
4 medium potatoes
Spanish extra Virgin olive oil
a drizzle of tabasco (optional)
salt to taste
aioli (see recipe on page 93)

1. Pre-heat oven to 200°C (392°F).
2. Pre-heat oven. Peel and wash the potatoes. Cut into irregular medium chunks.
3. Place them on a baking tray and season with salt.
4. Pour olive oil all over the potato chunks. Give them a toss with your hands.
5. Roast in the oven in middle rack until light golden and tender (about 20-30 minutes). Take out of the oven and place on plate or serving tray.
6. Make the aioli following recipe on page 79.
7. Add the tabasco sauce to the aioli and combine. Spoon the aioli over the potatoes

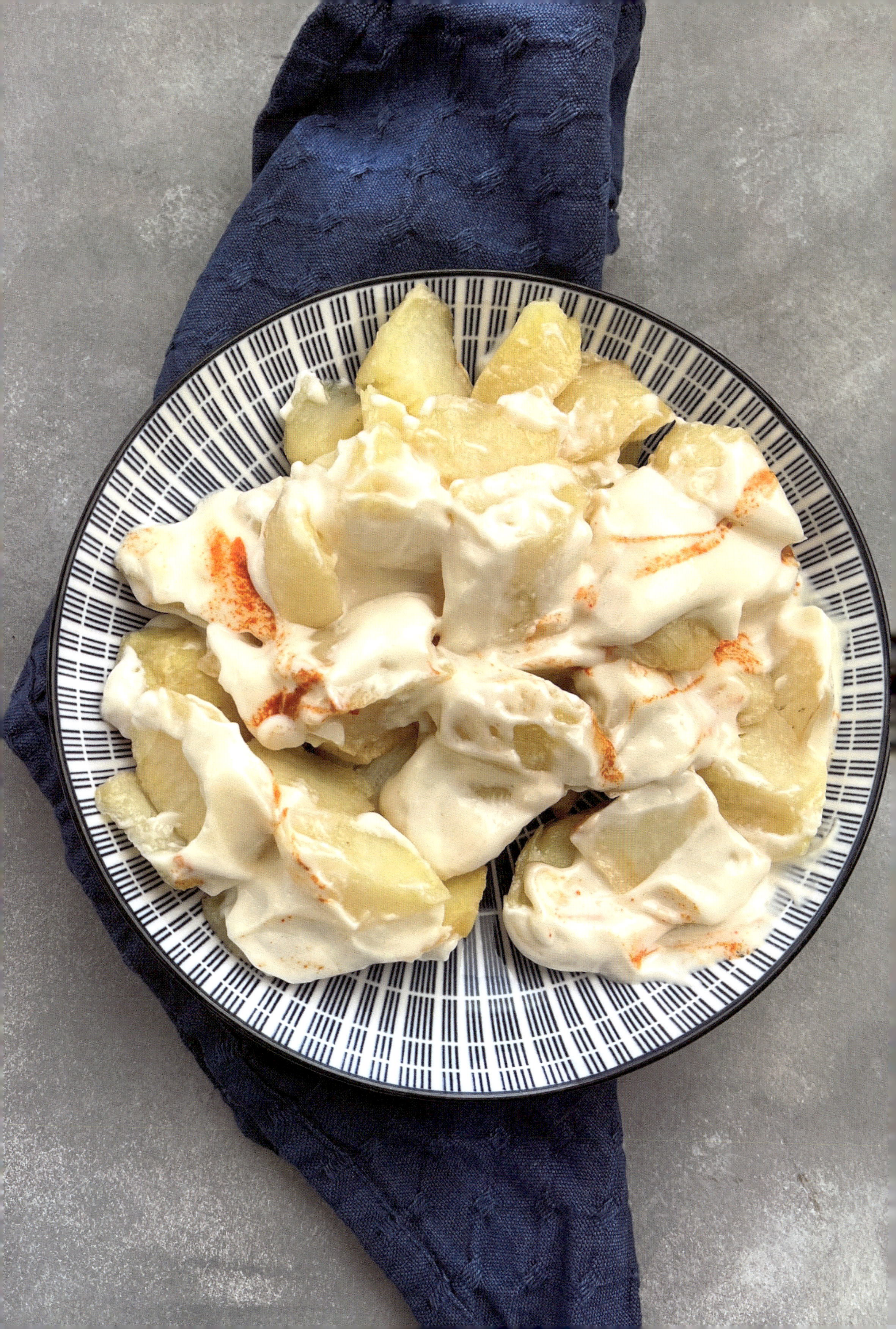

TAPAS

FUNGHI CROQUETTES Croquetas de setas

SERVES 4-6 PEOPLE:
300 gr. (10.5 oz.) funghi
1 garlic clove, finely minced
Spanish Virgin olive oil
Salt and pepper to taste

For the bechamel:
75 gr (2.6 oz.) butter/vegetable margarine
60 gr (2.1 oz.) corn flour
10 gr buckwheat flour
10 gr. chickpea flour
500 ml (2 cups) lactose free milk
Salt to taste
Ground black pepper to taste

For the batter:
2 beaten eggs
gluten-free breadcrumbs

1. Wash and press the mushrooms in your hand so the water in them comes out. Cut off their tails. Mince them up finely with a knife or with a mincer. Fry in a pan with oil along with the garlic cloves. Season with salt and pepper. Cook until tender and set aside. Prepare the bechamel following recipe on page 94
2. Once you´ve prepared the bechamel in a pot or saucepan, mix in the funghi. Cook covered for about 2 minutes.
3. Spoon the bechamel sauce onto a plate. Spread the mixture evenly. Let it cool for 30 minutes. Then you can either brush the surface with butter or cover it with cling film touching the surface. That will prevent the formation of a skin. Refrigerate for at least 1 hour.
4. Take the bechamel out of the fridge. Knead the bechamel with your hands so it has some elasticity back and you can work with it.
5. Prepare 2 plates: one with gluten-free breadcrumbs and another with 2 beaten eggs
6. Cut a small portion of the cold bechamel with a knife or spoon and place it on the plate with the breadcrumbs. Shape the croquettes into any shape and size you like (fingers, balls, oval shape…). Roll the croquette in the breadcrumbs, shaking off any excess.
7. Press the croquette on the plate with the beaten eggs and dip it. With a fork, roll it so it gets completely coated by the eggs.
8. Lift it, roll it in the breadcrumbs again coating it evenly.
9. Heat up a good amount of olive oil in a frying pan over a high-medium heat. The amount of oil depends on the size of the pan. The oil must cover the bottom half of the croquettes and be quite hot at first. When it's hot (but before getting smoky hot) place them carefully in the oil. Lower the heat to a medium heat. Fry them in small batches. Turn them gently, for about 2 minutes, or until they are golden on all sides.
10. Lift out the croquettes, holding them briefly over the pan to allow excess oil to drain, and transfer to a paper towel lined plate to drain further. Serve warm.

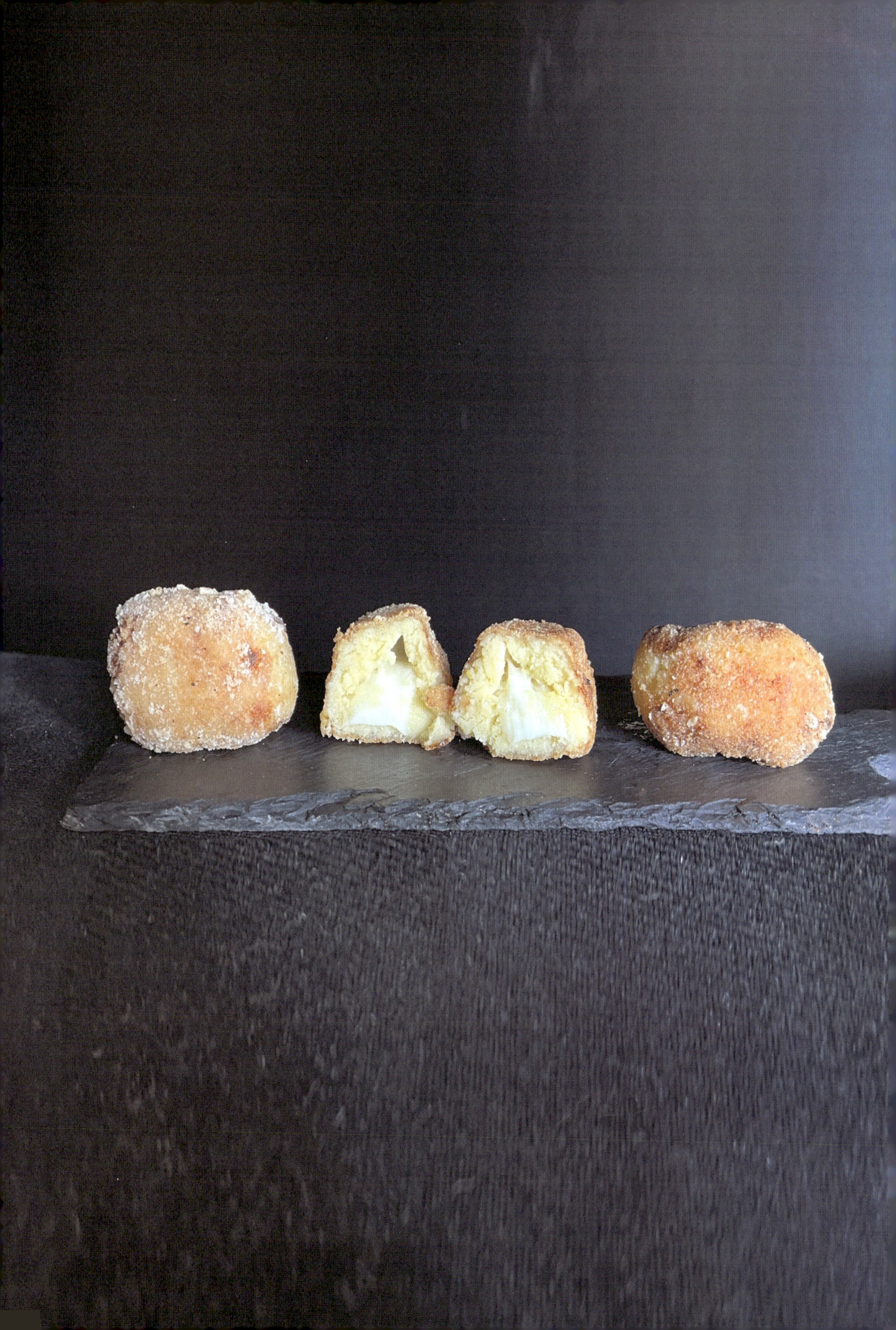

MANCHEGO CHEESE CROQUETTES
Croquetas de queso Manchego

These croquettes have the exact same ingredients and method as the Funghi croquettes. You just have to use 200 gr. (7 oz.) of grated Manchego cheese instead of funghi. Alternatively, you can cut long stripes of Manchego cheese and cover each stripe completely with thick bechamel (see photo below)

SPINACH CROQUETTES
Croquetas de espinacas

These croquettes have the exact same ingredients and method as the Funghi croquettes. Instead of funghi, you just have to use 300 gr. (7 oz.) of spinach cooked as follows: Heat 2 Tbsp. olive oil and fry the spinach stirring constantly. When the spinach has reduced considerably in size, mix in 1 finely minced garlic clove and 1 tsp. mustard and cook for 1-2 minutes, stirring well. Season with salt.

Desserts

DESSERTS

SANTIAGO CAKE Tarta de Santiago

The Santiago Cake happens to be a gluten free cake as it is made with ground almonds instead of flour. Isn't that great? But this is no ordinary almond cake. It's so moist, scrumptious and easy to make that you won't want to stop making it again and again. In my house, it doesn't last more than a day! This cake is very popular and well-known all over Spain but its origins are in the Galician city of Santiago de Compostela where the apostle Santiago's body lies. That is why it is usually marked with the shape of the cross of the Order of Santiago.

SERVE 6
250 gr. (8.8 oz.) raw almonds
5 large eggs
½ tsp. lemon zest
1/4 tsp. ground cinnamon
1 Tbsp. anisette
unsalted butter or oil to grease
250 gr. (8.8 oz.) powdered sugar + more to dust

1. Pre-heat oven to 120°C (250°F9. I like grinding the almonds in two batches. I grind the first batch very finely until I get a sort of "almond flour". I then grind the second batch less finely so that I can feel the almonds crunch between my teeth when eating the cake. Line an oven tray with baking paper and spread the ground almonds. Roast in the middle rack of the oven for 10 minutes.
2. In a large bowl, beat the sugar and eggs with a hand whisk into a pale cream. Beat in the zest, cinnamon and anisette. Let the roast almonds cool and then add them into the bowl, mixing well with a spatula.
3. Grease with butter a 9 inch (23 cm. approx.) spring form pan. Pour the cake mix into the pan and bake in middle rack in a pre-heated oven at 180°C (355 °F) for 35 minutes or until a needle comes out clean. Let it cool before un-molding.
4. Cut a cross of the Order of Santiago out of paper or thin cardboard. Place it on the cake and dust it with powdered sugar. Carefully remove the paper.

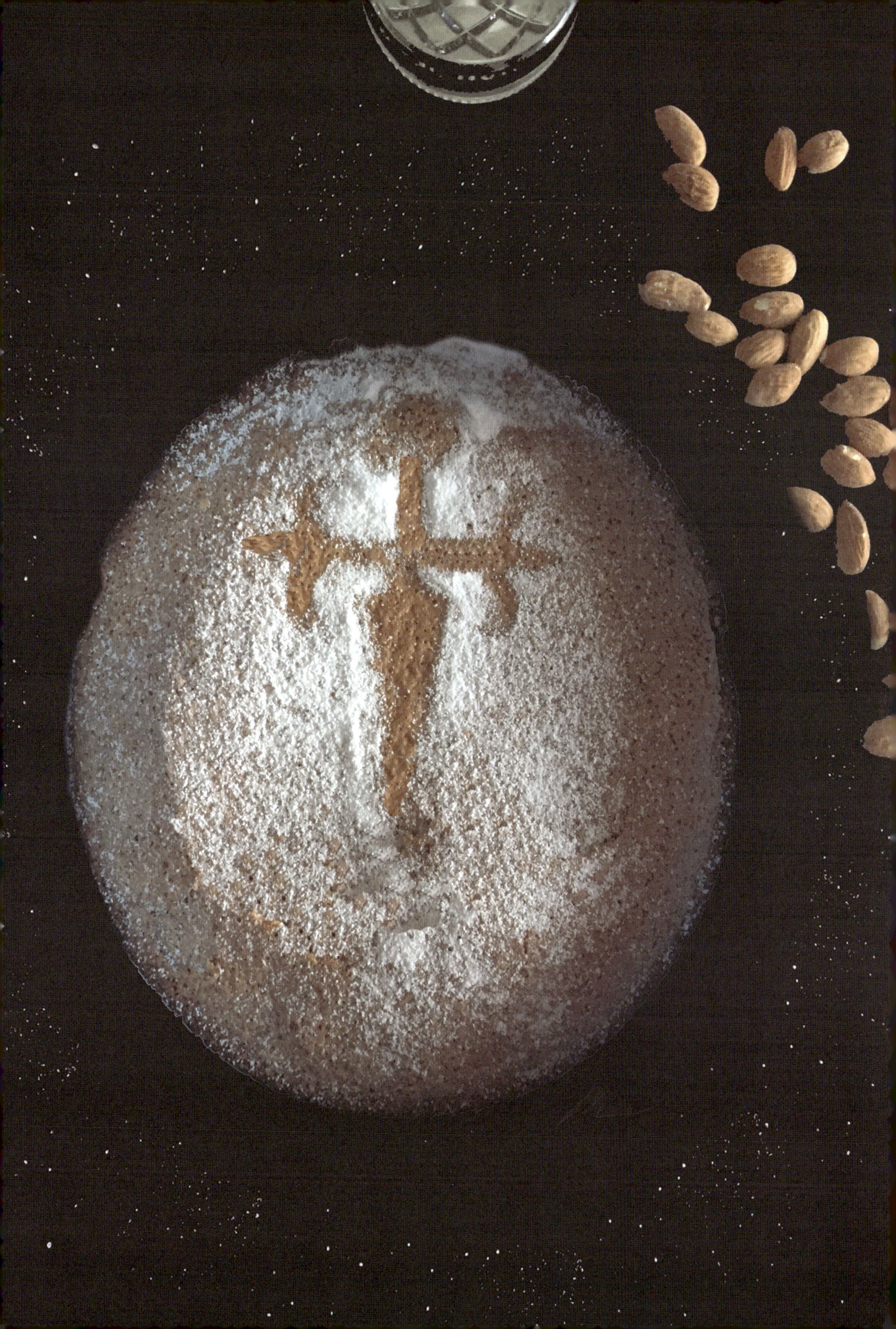

DESSERTS
HOMEMADE YOGHURT SPONGE CAKE
Bizcocho de yogur casero

This is a very popular recipe in Spanish homes. All measures are calculated with a 125 ml. (1/2 cup) empty yoghurt container. Really easy!

SERVES 8-10
(125 ml./1/2 cup) 1 natural flavor yoghurt
3 eggs
1 measure of corn flour, sifted
1 measure of chickpea, sifted

2 measures of sugar
1 measure of olive oil
15 gr. (1 Tbsp.). baking powder
a pinch of salt
powdered sugar for decoration

1. Put the sugar, eggs, yoghurt and oil in a free standing electric mixer with a paddle attachment (or use a whisk) and beat until ingredients are well incorporated. Add the sifted corn and chickpea flour, baking powder and salt a little at a time while beating. Beat until well mixed.
2. Pour the mixture into a 23 cm. (9 inch) baking tray, greased with a bit of oil.
3. Bake in the pre-heated oven at 170°C (325°F) for 20-25 min. or until golden brown and an inserted needle comes out clean. Let it cool before un-molding. Sprinkle powdered sugar on top.

TIP: Try different yoghurt flavors like lemon. You could also add in ¼ tsp. vanilla extract. You can also substitute the corn and chickpea flour with coconut flour.

SPANISH SWEET BREAD Torrijas

This is a sweet delicacy that Spaniards eat especially as a dessert or afternoon snack during Easter. It dates back to the 15th century and is believed to have been created in the convents to use up stale bread. There are many variations but here I'm going to show you the original recipe.

SERVES 6
12 slices of stale gluten-free crusty bread
500 ml. (2 cups) of milk
1 cinnamon stick
1 lemon peel
4 Tbsp. sugar

2 beaten eggs
2 Tbsp. buckwheat flour
2 Tbsp. corn flour
Tbsp. ground cinnamon
Spanish extra virgin olive oil

1. Cut the bread into slices approximately 3/4 of an inch (2 cm.) thick.
2. Heat the milk in a sauce pan over a medium-high heat. Add 2 Tbsp. of sugar, the lemon peel and cinnamon stick. Stir to dilute the sugar. Bring to boil and then remove from heat.
3. Pass the milk through a sieve. Place a bowl underneath it. Let it cool for 5-10 minutes.
4. Place the bread slices on a plate and with a spoon or a ladle, pour the milk from the bowl over each slice. Turn the bread over and pour milk over again to make sure the slices are completely soaked, even the crust. The inside of the bread should be mushy.
5. Start heating up a good amount of extra virgin olive oil in a small frying pan over a high-medium heat. Prepare a plate with the mix flour and another one with 2 beaten eggs. Coat each bread slice in the flour shaking off any excess. Dip both sides of the slices in the beaten eggs.
6. When the olive oil is hot, lower the heat to medium and start frying the torrijas. The oil should cover the bottom half of the bread. When the bottom of the bread begins to slightly brown (about 1 minute) turn them over.
7. Fry until golden on both sides. Take them out of the frying pan using a slotted spoon.
8. Transfer to a paper towel lined plate to drain the excess oil. Let them cool for 2 minutes.
9. Mix 2 Tbsp. of sugar with 1 Tbsp. of ground cinnamon in a small bowl or plate. Stir well with a fork. Coat the torrijas all over by rolling them in the sugar-cinnamon mixture. Serve and enjoy.

DESSERTS

DESSERTS

FRIED MILK Leche Frita

This recipe originally comes from Castilla la Mancha although other regions claim it. It has influences from the Arabs and it could be described as a very thick type of custard, battered and fried. It is eaten especially as a dessert or afternoon snack during Easter.

MAKES 8
500 ml. (2 cups) of warm milk
4 yolks
40 gr. (1.5 oz.) butter
50 gr. (1.8 oz.) corn flour

100 gr. (1/2 cup) sugar
Spanish extra Virgin olive oil
1 whole egg for the batter
2 Tbsp. corn flour for the batter
1 Tbsp. ground cinnamon

1. Separate the 4 eggs, placing the yolks in a large bowl and the whites in a small bowl. You can keep the whites to make other recipes like meringues

2. Whisk the yolks with the sugar until incorporated. Whisk in the warm milk.

3. Melt the butter in a saucepan over a medium-low heat. Stir in the corn flour and cook stirring constantly until is light golden. The flour has to be fried as the recipe will taste of uncooked flour if you don't do it.

4. Pour the contents of the bowl into the saucepan and set over a medium-low heat. Stir constantly and scrape the bottom of the pan at the same time with a wooden spatula. Don't let the creme boil because that would ruin it.

5. Keep on stirring and cook for 10 minutes or until it separates easily from the sides of the pan and a wooden spoon can stand up on its own in the middle. Remove from the heat.

6. Spoon the creme into a deep square/rectangular container. Spread the mixture evenly. It's got to be at least 1 cm (1/3 inch) thick. Refrigerate for 2-3 hours.

7. Prepare 2 plates: one with 2 Tbsp. corn flour and another with 1 beaten egg.

8. Cut a small square or rectangular portion of the creme with a knife. Roll in the flour, shaking off any excess. Press it on the plate with the beaten eggs. With a fork, roll it so it gets completely coated by the egg.

9. Heat up a good amount of olive oil in a frying pan over a high-medium heat. The amount of oil depends on the size of the pan. The oil must cover the bottom half of the portions and be quite hot at first. When it's hot (but before getting smoky hot) place them carefully in the oil. Lower the heat to a medium heat. Turn them gently, for about 2 minutes, or until they are golden on both sides.

10. Using a slotted spoon, lift them out, holding them briefly over the pan to allow excess oil to drain, and transfer to a paper towel lined plate to drain further. Cool for 2 minutes.

11. Mix 2 Tbsp. of sugar with 1 Tbsp. of ground cinnamon in a small bowl or plate. Stir well with a fork. Coat the portions by rolling them in the sugar-cinnamon mixture. Serve and enjoy.

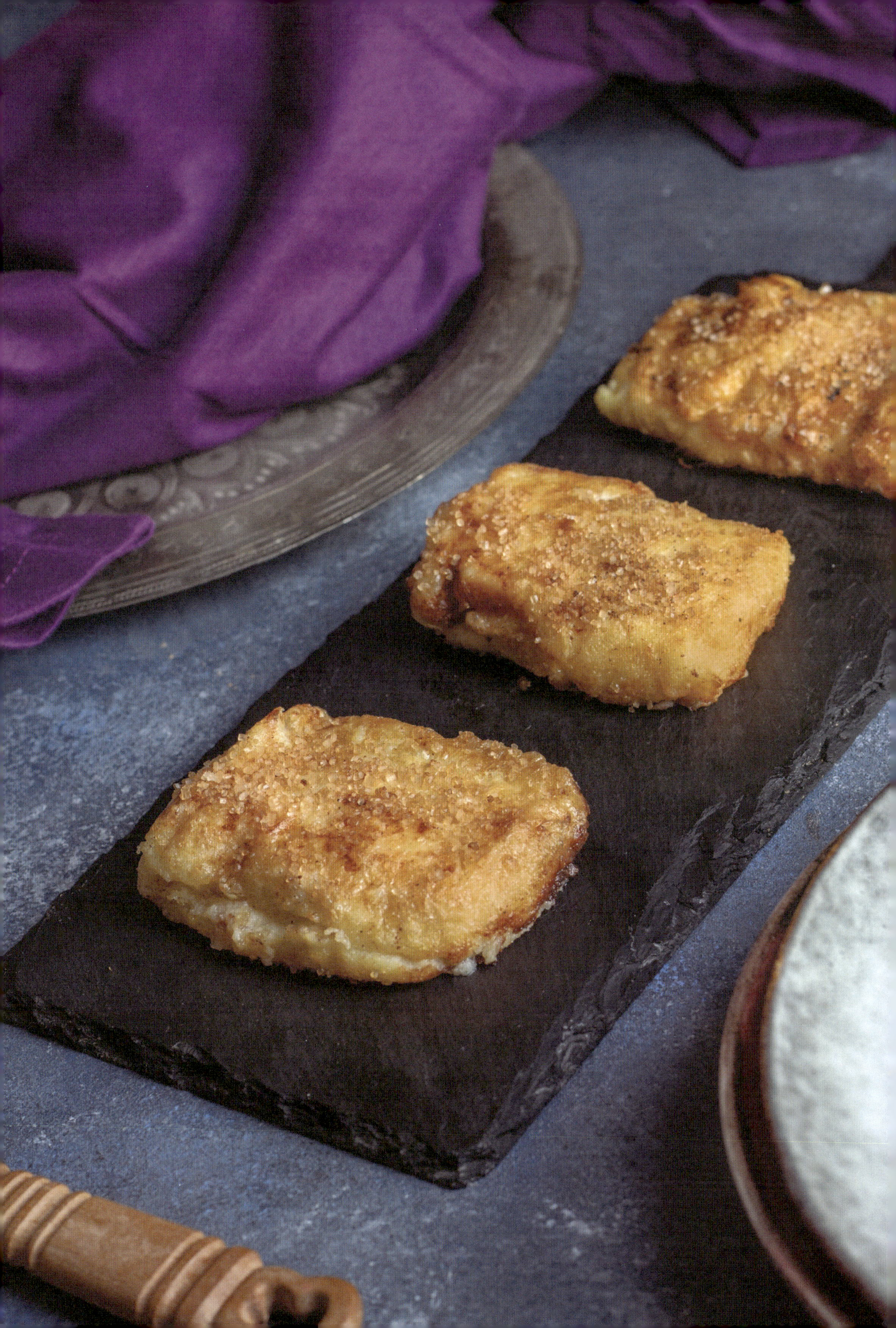

CANTABRIAN CHEESECAKE Quesada Pasiega

The term "Quesada" means cheesecake and "Pasiega" means from the Pas Valley which in Cantabria. It looks very different form the typical Anglo-Saxon cheesecake people are familiar with. This cheesecake is low in height and not creamy but it is really nice and unique.

SERVES 8-10:
500 gr. (17.5 oz.) requesón or cottage cheese if you can't find it
3 whole eggs
1 yolk
100 gr. (1/2 cup) melted butter
250 gr. (1 ¼ cups) sugar
80 gr. (2.8 oz) corn flour, sifted
grated lemon zest of ½ lemon
1/2 tsp. ground cinnamon
a pinch of salt
ground cinnamon and sugar to sprinkle the cake pan

1. In a large bowl, whisk the eggs and yolk, melted butter and sugar until well incorporated.

2. In another bowl, whisk the cottage cheese, cinnamon, lemon zest and salt. Pour into the large bowl with the egg mixture and mix well until fully incorporated.

3. Add the sifted corn flour little by little. Mix well until you get a creamy consistency.

4. Sprinkle sugar and cinnamon all over the base of the cake pan. Pour the mix into the cake pan. The cake pan must not have a removable bottom to avoid leaks and can have any shape you want. I use a 23 cm. (9 inch) diameter round cake pan.

5. Bake about 8 minutes at 200°C (375°F). Then, continue baking about 45 minutes at 180°C (355 °F). Serve warm.

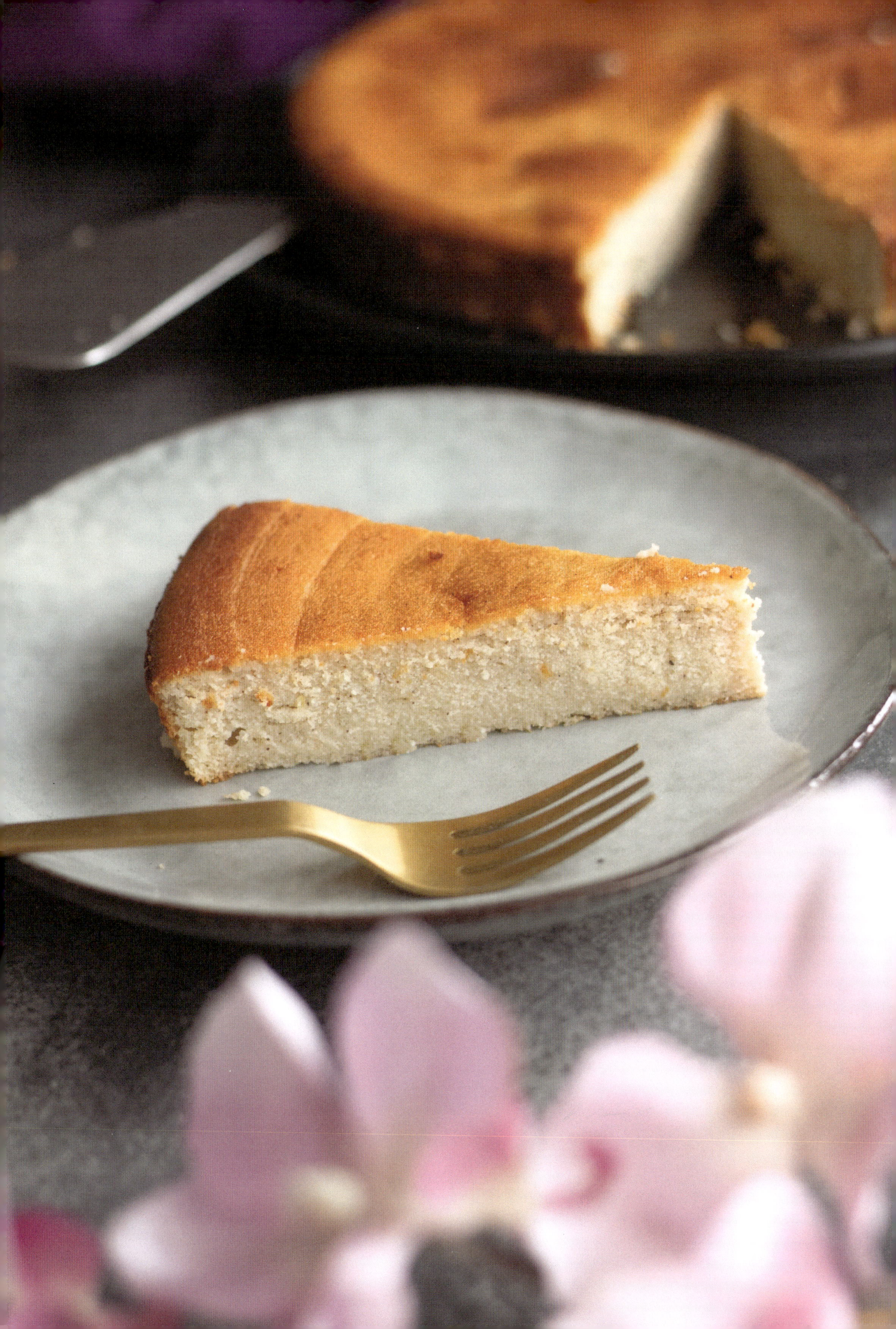

DESSERTS

ALMOND COOKIES Galletas almendradas

MAKES ABOUT 30 COOKIES :
300 gr. (2 ¾ cups) ground raw peeled or unpeeled almonds
3 eggs
grated lemon zest of 1 lemon
1 tsp. ground cinnamon
250 gr. (1 ¼ cups) sugar
¼ cup orujo liqueur or anisette if you can't find it
2 Tbsp. powdered sugar

1. Pre-heat oven to 190°C (375°F)

2. Put the ground almonds, eggs, lemon zest, cinnamon and sugar in a free-standing electric mixer or use a whisk and beat until ingredients are well incorporated. If the dough is not thick enough to be shaped into balls using wet hands, mix in more ground almonds until you get that consistency.

3. Shape into balls. Roll them in the orujo liqueur and then in the powdered sugar.

4. Place the balls in an oven tray lined with baking paper. Leave in the fridge for at least 30 minutes.

5. Bake in middle rack at 190°C (375°F) for 20-30 minutes or until golden. Take out of the oven and allow to cool. Serve.

MARZIPAN Mazapán

This is a very traditional Christmas treat. There is nothing more typical than having these sweets on Christmas Eve or Christmas day as dessert. This recipe dates back to the 13th century after the "Navas de Tolosa " war which created a shortage of wheat. The nuns in the "San Clemente" convent in Toledo invented this recipe to feed the poor using the ingredients they did have in abundance (sugar and almonds).

MAKES ABOUT 50 PIEECES:
550 gr. (19.5 oz) ground raw peeled almonds
350 gr. (1 ¾ cups) sugar
125 ml (1/2 cup) water
1 egg white
1 lemon zest, grated
1 whole beaten egg to brush

1. Heat the sugar and water over a medium-low heat in a pot stirring constantly. Once the sugar is dissolved, remove from the heat.

2. Place the ground almonds in a large bowl. Pour the water with the sugar onto the almonds. Stir in the lemon zest and egg white. Mix with a wooden spoon until you get a thick homogeneous dough. Cover the bowl with cling film and leave in the refrigerator overnight.

3. Take the dough out of the fridge. Wet your hands with water and shape the dough into different shapes: oval, balls, star, animal shapes, etc. You can also use a cutter for shapes.

4. Place the marzipan on an oven tray lined with baking paper. You can carve decorations with a toothpick.

5. Brush them with the beaten egg. Bake in middle rack in pre-heated oven at 200°C (390°F) with NO FAN for about 12 minutes or until golden. Take out of the oven and allow to cool. Serve.

CLASSIC PANELLETS

This recipe comes originally from Catalonia although it has become so popular that nowadays "Panellets" are very easy to find all over Spain in bakeries and supermarkets. They are typically eaten for "All Saints Day" (1ˢᵗ November) and usually accompanied with a glass of "Moscatel" (Spanish sweet wine).

INGREDIENTS FROM MARZIPAN RECIPE IN PREVIOUS PAGE
Whole almonds or glacé cherries for decoration

1. Follow recipe Marzipan steps 1-3 shaping into balls of 15 gr. (0.5 oz.) approx. each. Place a whole almond on top or a glacé cherry.

2. Brush them carefully with the beaten egg. Bake in middle-lower rack in pre-heated oven at 200°C (390°F) with NO FAN for about 12 minutes or until golden. Take out of the oven and allow to cool. Serve.

PANELLETS WITH PINE NUTS

These are the most popular type of panellets in Catalonia.

INGREDIENTS FROM MARZIPAN RECIPE IN PREVIOUS PAGE
1 beaten egg white for coating
A handful of pine nuts for coating

1. Follow recipe Marzipan steps 1-3 shaping into balls of 15 gr. (0.5 oz.) approx. each.

2. Place the pine nuts in a small bowl or plate.

3. Roll each ball in the beaten egg white and then coat in the pine nuts. Place the balls on an oven tray lined with baking paper.

4. Brush them carefully with the beaten egg. Bake in middle-lower rack in pre-heated oven at 200°C (390°F) with NO FAN for about 12 minutes or until golden. Take out of the oven and allow to cool. Serve.

PANELLETS WITH CHOPPED ALMONDS

1. Follow the recipe Panellets with pine nuts but instead of using pine nuts, use chopped almonds.

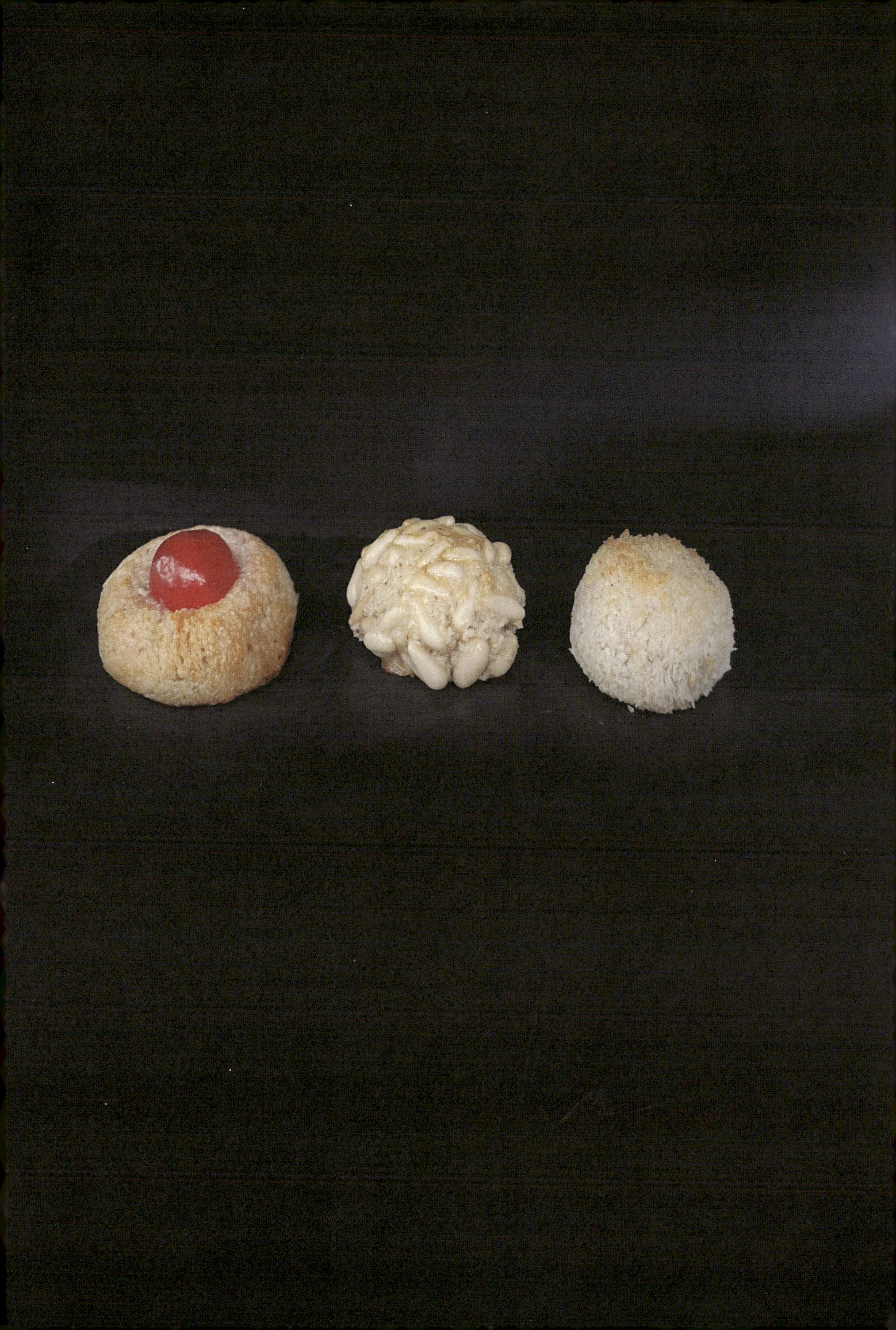

COCONUT PANELLETS

TO MAKE ABOUT 8 PANELLETS:
INGREDIENTS FROM MARZIPAN RECIPE IN PREVIOUS PAGE
2 Tbsp of finely grated coconut
1 beaten egg white for coating
2 Tbsp of grated coconut for coating

1. Follow recipe Marzipan steps 1-2

2. Take 100 gr. (3.5 oz) of marzipan dough and mix it with 1 Tbsp. grated coconut using your hands. The measurements are approximate and can be changed according to your taste.

3. Wet your hands and shape into small balls of 15 gr. (0.5 oz.) approx. each.

4. Place 1 Tbsp. grated coconut in a small bowl or plate.

5. Roll each ball in the beaten egg white and then coat in the grated coconut. Place the balls on an oven tray lined with baking paper.

6. Bake in middle-lower rack in pre-heated oven at 200°C (390°F) with NO FAN for about 12 minutes or until golden. Take out of the oven and allow to cool. Serve.

COFFEE PANELLETS

TO MAKE ABOUT 8 PANELLETS:
INGREDIENTS FROM MARZIPAN RECIPE IN PREVIOUS PAGE
1 Tbsp of ground coffee

1. Follow recipe Marzipan steps 1-2

2. Take 100 gr. (3.5 oz) of marzipan dough and mix it with 1 Tbsp. ground coffee using your hands. The measurements are approximate and can be changed according to your taste.

3. Wet your hands and shape into a large coffee bean shape of 15 gr. (0.5 oz.) approx. each.

4. Brush them carefully with the beaten egg. Bake in middle-lower rack in pre-heated oven at 200°C (390°F) with NO FAN for about 12 minutes or until golden. Take out of the oven and allow to cool. Serve.

5. Bake in middle rack in pre-heated oven at 200°C (390°F) for about 12 minutes or until golden. Take out of the oven and allow to cool. Serve.

LITTLE SIGHS Suspiros Merenguitos

MAKES ABOUT 8 LARGE SIGHS:
4 (2/3 cup) egg whites
a pinch of salt
350 gr. (1 ½ cup) fine sugar

1. Put the egg whites and a pinch of salt in a free-standing electric mixer with a whisk attachment. On a medium-low speed, whisk until frothy (about 2 minutes).

2. Increase the speed to high and add the sugar gradually, 2 Tbsp. at a time. Whisk until stiff peaks form and looks glossy.

3. Put the meringue in a piping bag with a star shape nozzle and form swirls on a paper lined baking tray.

4. Bake in pre-heated oven at 120°C (250°F) for 40-60 minutes or until completely dry.

ALMOND SIGHS
Merenguitos de almendra

MAKES ABOUT 8 LARGE SIGHS:
4 (2/3 cup) egg whites
a pinch of salt
350 gr. (1 ½ cup) fine sugar
180 gr. (1 1/3 cup) roasted peeled ground almond
1 Tbsp. lemon juice
1 tsp. grated lemon zest
½ tsp. ground cinnamon (optional)

1. Put the egg whites and a pinch of salt in a free-standing electric mixer with a whisk attachment. On a medium-low speed, whisk until frothy (about 2 minutes).

2. Increase the speed to high and add the sugar gradually, 2 Tbsp. at a time. Whisk in the lemon juice. Whisk until stiff peaks form.

3. Whisk in the lemon zest and cinnamon until well integrated.

4. Spoon the almonds into the meringue. Mix carefully with a silicon spatula with circular movements.

5. Put the meringue in a piping bag with a star shape nozzle and form swirls on a paper lined baking tray.

6. Bake in pre-heated oven at 140°C (285°F) for 30-40 minutes or until they start to crackle.

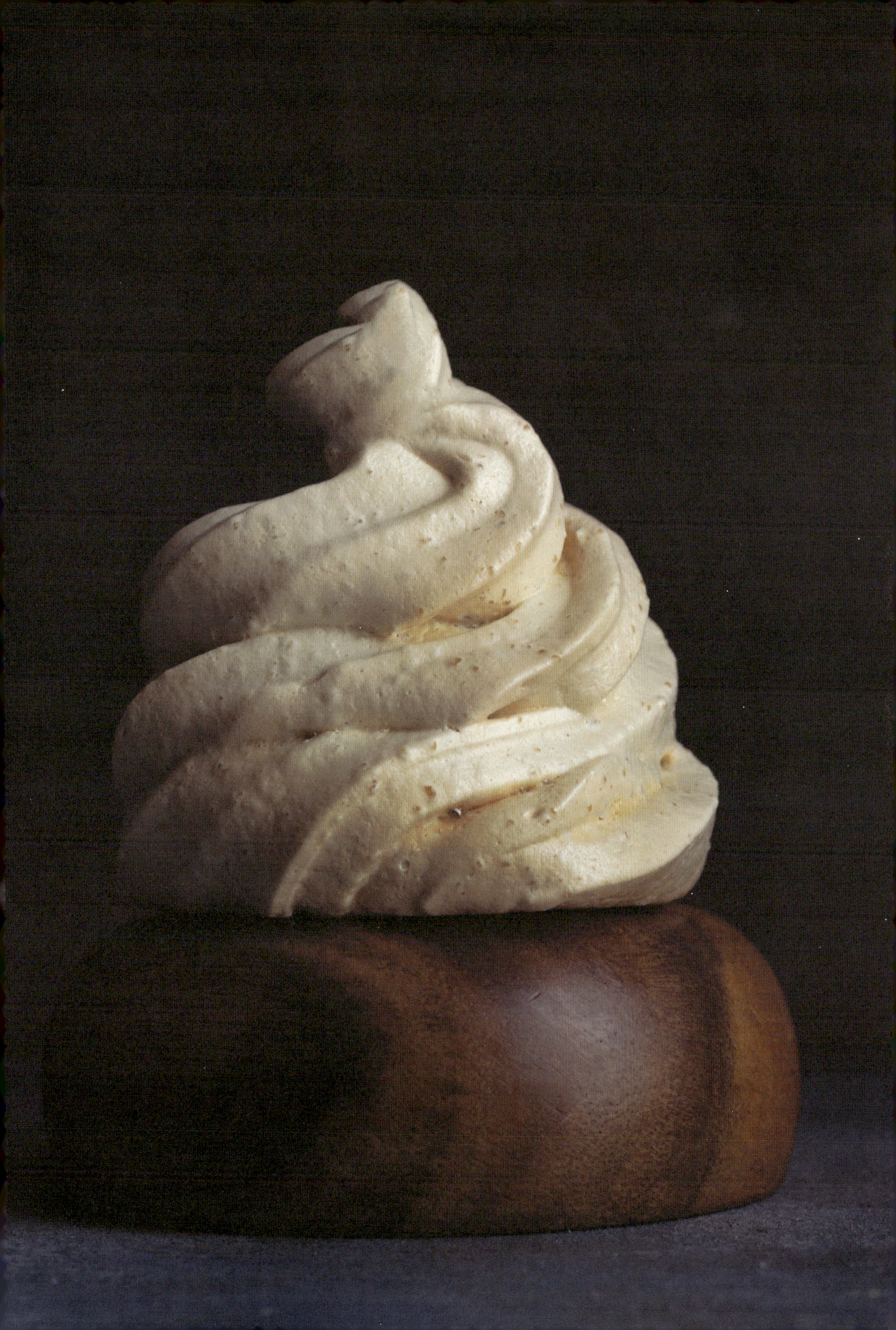

DESSERTS

EGG FLAN Flan de huevo

There's nothing better than finishing a great Spanish meal with this fantastic dessert. It is originally from Spain but has influenced many Latin-American gastronomies. It's a classic and one of the most popular desserts served everywhere in Spain. Beware that the traditional authentic Spanish recipe has no vanilla extract.

SERVES 6-8
4 eggs
4 Tbsp. granulated sugar
500 ml. (2 cups milk)
whipped cream (optional)
6 Tbsp. water
200 gr. (1 cup) granulated sugar for the caramel

1. Pre-heat oven to 190°C (374°F).
2. To make the caramel, bring to a boil 200 gr. (1 cup) of sugar and 3 Tbsp. of water in a saucepan over high heat, without stirring until liquefied and amber in color. While the sugar boils, occasionally brush the inner sides of the pot with water, to keep the sugar from crystallizing.
3. You have 2 options:
   A) Prepare individual flans for each person. You should use ramekins.
   B) Prepare the Flan in one large flan dish.
4. Quickly pour the caramel into the ramekins or flan dish before the caramel gets hard.
5. Break 4 eggs in a large bowl. Beat the eggs with 4 Tbsp. of sugar.
6. Pour in the milk and whisk until smooth with a hand whisk. Pour bowl mixture into the ramekins.
7. Pour water into a large deep baking tray to prepare a "bain mare" boiling water bath. Cover the ramekins with foil and place in the water. The water must cover the bottom half of the ramekins. Bake in pre-heated oven 45-60 min. or until a needle comes out clean when inserted. Be sure to carefully keep the water level topped up while they are in the oven.
8. Let cool at room temperature for 20 minutes. Then chill thoroughly in refrigerator for at least 2 hours. When ready to serve, un-mold by running a knife around the inside edge of each ramekin.
9. Place a plate on top of the ramekin.
10. With one hand under the ramekin and the other on top of the plate, turn over. Tap the ramekin and the flan should drop onto the plate. If it doesn't, carefully "prod" the flan out of the ramekin with a small paring knife. It should slide out.
11. In Spain, it is usually served with whipped cream.

SPANISH CUSTARD Natillas

Homemade Spanish custard is quite different from English custard. The Spanish one is thinner and has a rich tea biscuit on top. Cinnamon is also frequently used which adds a typical Spanish twist. It can keep in the fridge for up to 3 days.

MAKES 4-5
4 egg yolks
2 Tbsp. granulated sugar
1 Tbsp. vanilla sugar
1 Tbsp. cornflour
600 ml. (1 pint) whole milk
ground cinnamon
4 rich gluten-free tea biscuits or similar

1. Separate the eggs, placing the yolks in a large basin and the whites in a small bowl. You can keep the white to make other recipes like meringues.
2. Whisk the yolks. Add the sugar, vanilla sugar and corn flour to the beaten yolks and stir well.
3. Add 2 Tbsp. of milk and whisk into a smooth paste.
4. In a saucepan, heat the remaining milk until scalding hot and about to boil. Pour slowly into the egg mixture in the basin, whisking vigorously as you go.
5. Return it to the saucepan and set over a low heat until it thickens. Stir constantly and scrape the bottom of the pan at the same time with a wooden spatula. Don't let the custard boil because that will ruin it. It'll be ready when the foam around the borders disappears. This can take up to 10 minutes.
6. Pour it into a bowl and let it cool for 10 minutes.
7. If you see the custard has curdled or you find bits in it, take them out with a sieve spoon or pass through a sieve.
8. Pour into individual containers using a ladle. Refrigerate for at least 2 hours.
9. Place the biscuits on top after the custard has refrigerated for 30 minutes. Just before serving, sprinkle ground cinnamon on top.

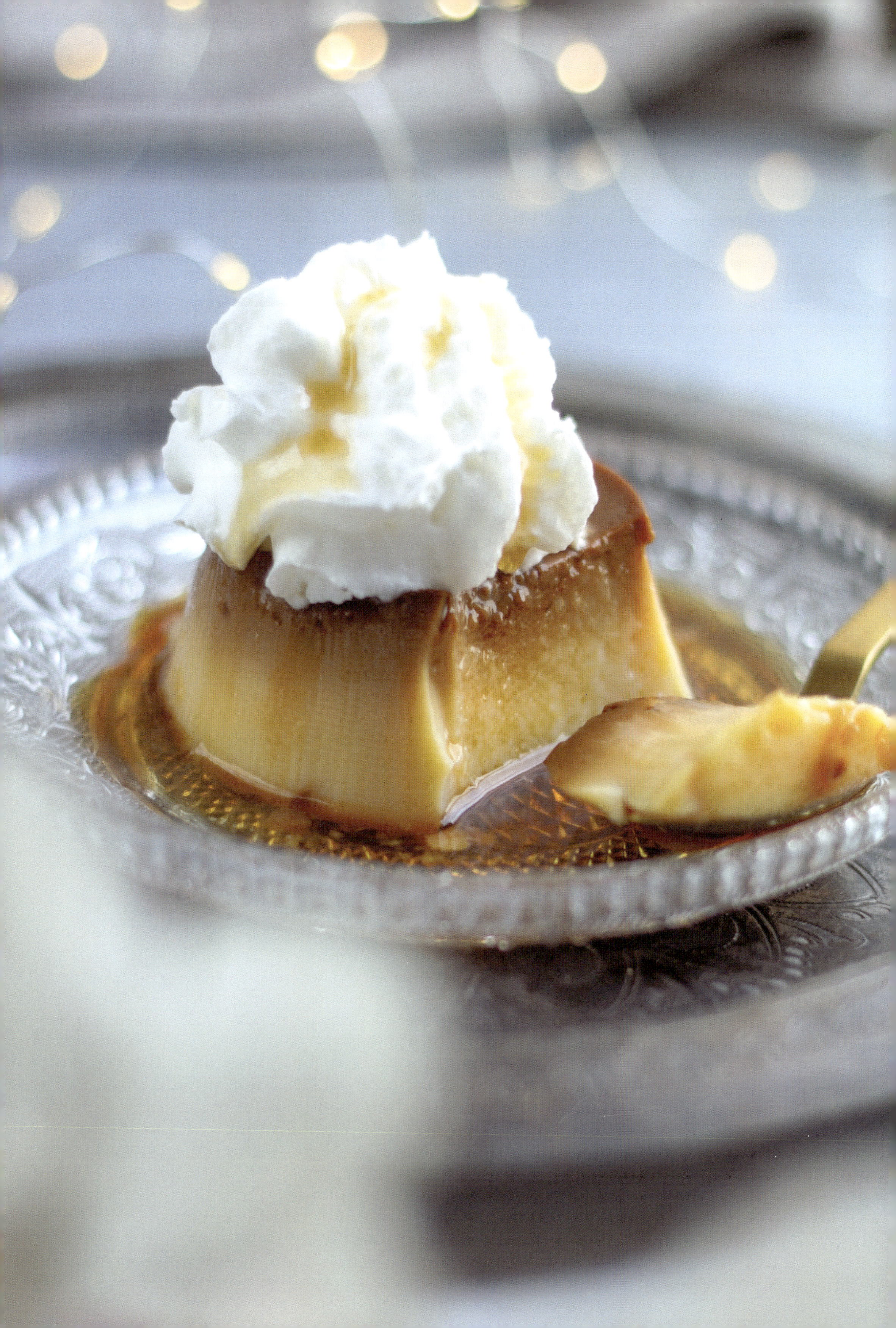

CATALAN CRÈME BRÛLÉE

Crema Catalana

This dessert is very similar to the French Crème Brûlée but this one is infused with citrus flavor. It appears regularly on every Spanish restaurant menu and originates from the 18th century when nuns in a convent in Catalonia prepared a flan for a bishop that was too runny. They tried to fix it by adding a layer of burnt sugar and when the Bishop tried it he yelled: "Crema!" meaning in Catalan: "It burns!".

SERVES 4-6
1 liter (4 cups) whole milk
6 large egg yolks
45 gr. (3 Tbsp.) corn flour
100 gr. (1 cup) granulated sugar +sugar to caramelize

half an orange peel
half a lemon peel
1 cinnamon stick

1. Heat the milk with the cinnamon stick, the orange and lemon peel in a saucepan until scalding hot and about to boil. Remove from the heat, cover with a lid and let it set for at least 30 minutes.

2. Separate the eggs, placing the yolks in a large bowl and the whites in a small bowl. You can keep the whites to make other recipes like meringues. Whisk the yolks with the sugar until incorporated. Whisk in the corn flour.

3. Pour the milk infusion slowly into the egg mixture in the large bowl, while passing through a sieve. Whisk until well combined.

4. Pour the contents of the bowl into a saucepan and set over a low heat. Cook until it thickens, stirring constantly and scraping the bottom of the pan at the same time with a wooden spatula. Don't let the creme boil because that would ruin it.

5. If you see the creme has curdled or you find bits in it, take the bits out with a sieve spoon or pass the creme through a sieve.

6. Pour into individual containers using a ladle. Refrigerate for at least 4 hours (preferably overnight). The typical containers used in Catalonia are made of clay. Sprinkle a layer of granulated sugar and caramelize with a kitchen torch just before serving.

REFERENCE RECIPES

REFERENCE RECIPES

VEGETABLE BROTH Caldo de Verduras

1'5 liters (6 cups) of water
1 leek
2 garlic cloves
1 small onion
2 carrots

2 ripe tomatoes
4 sprigs of parsley
1 bay leaf
2 Tbsp. Spanish extra Virgin olive oil
sea salt to taste

1. Cut the garlic cloves in half. Chop the rest of the vegetables. In a large tall pot, heat the olive oil and fry the leek, onion and garlic cloves over a medium heat for 5 minutes, stirring frequently. Stir in the carrots and bay leaf over and continue cooking for 3 minutes. Mix in the tomatoes, parsley and salt. Fry for 10 minutes, stirring frequently.
2. Pour in the water. Bring to boil and cook covered for 30-45 minutes.
3. Remove from heat and pass through a sieve.
4. Let it cool in a bowl.

MAYONNAISE Mayonesa

METHOD 1. BY HAND (SERVES 6-8)
2 egg yolks at room temperature
½ liter (2 cups) olive oil
½ tsp. vinegar or lemon juice a pinch of salt

1. Place the egg yolks and salt in a ceramic bowl or mortar. Stir with a whisk, pestle or fork.
2. Then, slowly drizzle a drop of oil while whisking vigorously until you see the oil has been absorbed. Slowly, pour more oil (a small amount) little by little while whisking. Continue drizzling oil and whisking until you've used up all the oil. You'll see how an emulsion starts to form that will turn into mayonnaise at the end.
3. Once it's ready, stir in 1/2 tsp. of vinegar or lemon juice and adjust salt if needed.

METHOD 2. WITH IMMERSION (STICK) BLENDER (SERVES 4)
1 egg at room temperature
1/4 tsp. vinegar or lemon juice
250 ml. (1 cup) olive oil
a pinch of salt

1. Place the egg, olive oil, vinegar and salt in a tall container. Insert the immersion blender switched off in the container. Push the head of the blender onto the bottom and then switch it on, on slow speed. Don't move it for about 5-10 seconds (depending on the blender power).
2. When you see the ingredients turn into a sort of thick mayonnaise (with the immersion blender still on) move the blender slowly up and down until you get a mayonnaise mixture.

REFERENCE RECIPES

EGG AIOLI Allioli con huevo

You can follow any of the 2 Mayonnaise Methods on this page. You just have to add one peeled crushed garlic clove at the beginning of either of the recipes. You can crush it with either a garlic crusher or a mortar and pestle. Do not add any vinegar or lemon juice at the end.

One important tip, if you don't digest raw garlic very well: remove the core by doing the following: Peel the garlic and cut it lengthwise. Insert the knife and remove the small long core that is in the middle. Yes. It´s that simple!

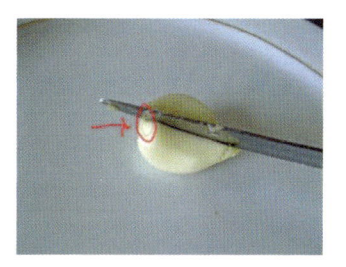

GENUINE AIOLI Allioli

Genuine aioli is made only with garlic, salt and olive oil. It can only be made using a mortar and pestle.

MAKES ABOUT 1 1/2 CUP
10 garlic cloves
a pinch of salt
Spanish extra Virgin olive oil

1. Peel the garlic cloves and crush in a mortar with salt. Crush with the pestle until you get a smooth paste.
2. Pour a drop of olive oil slowly into the mortar while you turn the pestle in slow circular motions. When the paste soaks up the oil, pour a very short drizzle of oil while turning the pestle until the paste soaks up the oil again.
3. Pour a longer thin drizzle of oil and repeat turning the pestle. Repeat this process making the drizzle longer each time.
4. It is important that you turn the pestle in wide circular motions while pouring the oil. You will be able to turn the pestle a bit faster every time you pour olive oil. Keep adding the oil until you have the consistency of a thick mayonnaise. This will take about 20 minutes.

REFERENCE RECIPES

CLASSIC BECHAMEL

This recipe is used for lasagnas, manicotti, cannelloni and other pasta. It can be apt for vegans if vegetable margarine and vegetable milk is used

80 gr (2.8 oz.) butter/vegetable margarine
60 gr (2.1 oz.) corn flour
5 gr buckwheat flour
5 gr. chickpea flour
600 ml (2 ½ cups) lactose free milk or vegetable milk of your choice
salt to taste
Ground black pepper to taste

1. Heat the oil, margarine or butter in a medium size pan or sauce pan over a medium-high heat.
2. Add flour and fry, stirring until mixture is fried (golden), about 1 minute.
3. Add the milk in one go and whisk until smooth. The colder the milk, the less chance of having lumps in the bechamel. Cook over a high heat, whisking until the sauce comes to a boil. Then, reduce to a medium-low heat. Keep on stirring and cook until it thickens (about 6 minutes). Season with salt almost at the end. You want the bechamel to be creamy but not runny. If the bechamel doesn't thicken enough, you can try adding a crushed boiled egg yolk but I recommend frying flour in olive oil in another small pan and adding it into the bechamel. Don't add flour without frying it as the bechamel will taste of uncooked flour.

THICK BECHAMEL

This recipe is used for mainly for croquettes and stuffed boiled eggs. It can be apt for vegans if vegetable margarine and vegetable milk is used

80 gr (2.8 oz.) butter/vegetable margarine
60 gr (2.1 oz.) corn flour
10 gr buckwheat flour
10 gr. chickpea flour
500 ml (2 cups) lactose free milk or vegetable milk of your choice
salt to taste and ground black pepper to taste

1. Heat margarine or butter in a medium saucepan over a medium-high heat until melted.
2. Add the flour mix and fry, stirring until mixture is fried (golden), for about 1 minute. There's got to be enough flour so the melted butter can't take any more flour.
3. Add the milk in one go and whisk until smooth. The colder the milk, the less chance of having lumps in the bechamel. Cook over a high heat, whisking until the sauce comes to a boil. Reduce to a medium-low heat. Season with salt. Keep on stirring and cook until it thickens enough so it separates from the pan and looks like thick lava. Take into account that it will thicken considerably once it has been chilled in the fridge for 1 hour. If the bechamel doesn't thicken enough, you can try adding a crushed boiled egg yolk but I recommend frying flour in olive oil in another small pan and adding it into the bechamel. Don't add flour without frying it as the bechamel will taste of uncooked flour.

Printed in Great Britain
by Amazon